Kai Curry-Lindahl

A Chanticleer Press Edition

WILDLIFE OF THE PRAIRIES AND PLAINS

HARRY N. ABRAMS, INC., PUBLISHERS, NEW YORK

First frontispiece. *Black-tailed prairie dogs* (Cynomys ludovicianus) *are burrowing rodents that live in huge communities on North American prairies.*

Second frontispiece. *A lioness* (Panthera leo) *stalks through the grasses on the plains of Namibia, South-West Africa. Lions are true grasslands animals in Africa, where they are still common in many places although dwindling in others.*

Third frontispiece. *Giraffes* (Giraffa camelopardalis) *survey the savanna landscape of Cameroon, west-central Africa. Their long necks enable them to browse in the tree tops, at a height no other hoofed animal can reach. Thus they have a ready source of food all to themselves.*

Overleaf. *A common myna* (Acridotheres tristis) *hops a ride on an axis deer* (Cervus axis) *of Indian grassland. Mynas are very abundant in much of southern Asia. They occasionally feed near herd animals, looking for insects stirred up by the larger beasts. Axis deer sometimes gather in herds that number as many as 100 animals.*

Library of Congress Cataloging in Publication Data
Curry-Lindahl, Kai
Wildlife of the prairies and plains.
"A Chanticleer Press edition."
1. Prairie ecology. 2. Grassland ecology.
I. Title.
QH541.5.P7C87   574.5'2643   80-27927
ISBN 0-8109-1766-1

Color reproductions by Fontana & Bonomi, Milan, Italy
Composition by Dix Typesetting Co. Inc., Syracuse, New York
Printed and bound by Kingsport Press, Kingsport, Tennessee

Prepared and produced by Chanticleer Press, Inc., New York:
Publisher: Paul Steiner
Editor-in-Chief: Milton Rugoff
Managing Editor: Gudrun Buettner
Series Editor: Mary Suffudy
Assistant Editor: Ann Hodgman
Marketing: Carol Robertson
Production: Helga Lose, Dean Gibson
Art Associates: Carol Nehring, Deirdre F. McBreen
Appendixes, art: Dolores R. Santoliquido
Picture Library: Joan Lynch, Edward Douglas
Map: H. Shaw Borst
Design: Massimo Vignelli

Project consultant: Edward R. Ricciuti

Appendixes, text: pp. 194–209, 223–226 by David M. Sutherland, Professor of Biology, The University of Nebraska at Omaha; pp. 210–222 by John L. Paradiso, Senior Biologist, Office of Endangered Species, U.S. Fish and Wildlife Service

Note: Illustrations are numbered according to the pages on which they appear.

Contents

Preface

Grassland communities represent one of the earth's major biomes, ranging from tropical woodland savannas to temperate steppes, from tallgrass plains to shortgrass prairies. They include the savannas of tropical Africa, the floodplains of Asia, the steppes of the Ukraine, the high plateaus of Mongolia, the kangaroo grasslands of Australia, the llanos, campos, and pampas of South America, and the prairies of North America.

Grasslands pass by gradual stages into semi-deserts. In fact, many deserts are man-made: not long ago they were productive natural grasslands that have since deteriorated due to overutilization. Many of today's deserts and semi-deserts are still potential grasslands, and many grasslands are, in turn, potential forests. Both can recover if they are not continuously overexploited.

Some shrublands and scrublands of the world may also be included among grasslands. This type of bush and brush country occupies a large portion of Australia and is also widespread in Asia, Africa, and South America. Large tracts of semiarid areas in North America support vegetation which is predominantly sagebrush with patches of grasses.

It is remarkable how productive grasslands once were. They were the basis for early civilizations. The grassland biome was for millennia a perfectly balanced ecological system which offered optimal conditions for life.

Man himself has been intimately related to grasslands ever since he emerged from the forests of Africa about three million years ago. Despite this long experience modern man has failed to understand the ecology of savannas, steppes, and prairies. He has devastated few other biotic regions as thoroughly as these—changing the nature of the land through extermination and the introduction of exotics; overcultivating and overstocking without regard for the capacity of the environment. In the Old World, the destruction has gone so far that in many regions it appears to be irreversible. In the New World man has had less time for destructive work, so damage there may be reparable through sound range management.

Today, agricultural or pastoral economies characterize these grasslands. Has this change of land use led to an increased productivity on a sustained-yield basis and to the long-term benefit of man? The reply cannot be a simple "yes" or "no," because not all grasslands respond in the same way to man and his livestock. Grasslands in temperate areas are less vulnerable to misuse than are those in subtropical and tropical regions. However, where grasslands are continuously taxed by cultivation, fires, grazing, trampling, and other forms of utilization, they deteriorate at an accelerating rate. Unfortunately, this is happening everywhere, and especially in subtropical and tropical regions. In these often arid and semiarid areas, considerable portions of the grasslands are marginal in the sense that they are not suitable for agriculture or animal husbandry. But they were, and in some places still are, extremely productive in the form of wild animals which convert the grasses and bushes to proteins useful to man.

When looking at the present state of the world's grasslands, it is essential to bear in mind the important role the grassland vegetation plays in stabilizing the water cycle and preserving the soil, and the fact that grasslands, in turn, cannot exist without either of these renewable resources. They form a very complex pyramid of interrelationships. When man destroys one or several of the components, the pyramid collapses. If the grassland vegetation is destroyed, the fertile soil layer disappears. When the vegetation dies, so do the animals. When the country thus grows sterile, human communities nearby cannot survive. Some of today's deserts are silent memorials to a flourishing civilization that two to three thousand years ago was based on extremely fertile grasslands supporting important animal and human populations.

The wild fauna is also a vital natural resource. Irreplaceable biological treasures—chiefly mammals and birds—are gone forever because their habitats were altered or completely destroyed, or the animals themselves were killed off without thought of their value as a natural resource.

Man must learn to coexist with natural marginal lands and to restore the man-made ones to their former wealth, measured in terms of productivity. The conservatism of agriculturalists unwilling to recognize that animals other than a few domesticated species are a potential resource is distressing. In dealing with crop cultivation and livestock grazing on marginal lands, they always presume that wildlife is in conflict with them and must retreat, and that expansion of animal husbandry is always progress. This is a highly dangerous philosophy that has already caused the loss of enormous areas of productive land. It is increasingly important to get rid of unrealistic and conventional criteria for development of marginal lands. Effective utilization must include what these areas already produce: wild vegetation and wild animals that provide meat, hides, and other products.

The wild animals of the world's grasslands are too numerous and diverse in species to be considered in detail in a one-volume work. For example, in tropical Africa (that is, south of the Sahara) live 75 species of bovids (just one family of antelopes, sheep, and goats), while in Eurasia there are 27 species of this family and in North America 4 species. Most of them live on grasslands. There are even more of rodents and insectivores.

A giant restoration plan for the world's formerly productive, animal-yielding rangelands must be worked out and implemented before these areas have been irreversibly destroyed and the wild animal resources gone forever.

I am grateful to Paul Steiner and Gudrun Buettner for making this book possible and to Milton Rugoff, Mary Suffudy, and Edward Ricciuti, who contributed to the editing, selection of photographs, and art work.

Kai Curry–Lindahl

Grasslands exist on every
continent except Antarctica. They
range in character from those so
barren and arid that they verge
on desert—as in central Asia and
Australia—to those mixed with
forest—as on the eastern prairies
of North America and in parts of
Africa.

Landscapes of boundless
horizons, grasslands of all types
—even those that are seemingly
bleak—share an abundance of
life. The living organisms of
grasslands exploit the air, the
surface, and the soil. There is
more bulk by far in roots and
rhizomes beneath the surface than
in the leaves of grass above it. Yet
the leaves absorb sunlight and
carry on the photosynthesis
necessary for growth of the grass.
Spreading themselves far and
wide, grasses send their pollen

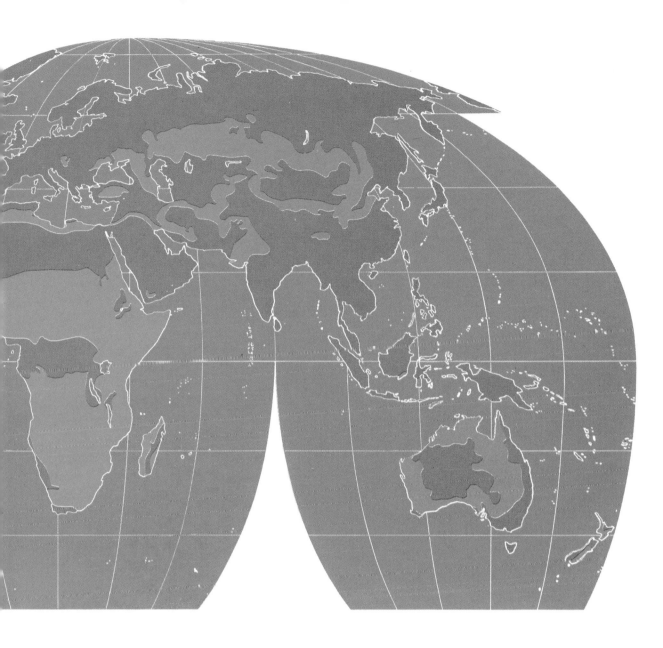

and seeds on the wind, expanding
the grassy kingdom through the
air.

Large grasslands can support
immense assemblages of wild
animals. They are home to herds
of elephant, bison, antelope, and
deer, and to the predators which
feed on them. Less obvious, but
just as important in the natural
scheme of things are the myriad
smaller creatures —such as
rodents, insectivores and
invertebrates —that live in and
under the grasses.

Overhead, birds swoop and soar
in search of the smaller animals.
Together, all these creatures with
the grasses that ultimately
support them, make up one of the
most important natural
relationships on earth.

A World of Grasses

People the world over call grasslands by different names —savannas, steppes, prairies, pampas, llanos, veldt, and plains. The variation is due not only to language differences but to the existence of several types of grasslands. A very widespread type of habitat, they constitute about 27 percent of the earth's natural vegetation, covering parts of all continents except Antarctica.

Whatever their type, grasslands survive basically by virtue of low humidity. Temperature, soil, and geology also play a role in determining the destiny of grasslands, as do animals and human beings, but most important is moisture. Stated simply, if more moisture falls on the landscape than evaporates from it, grasslands cannot exist. Natural grasslands—as opposed to those which come about through human agency—can be thought of as an intermediate environment between the moist forest and the dry desert realms.

It is sometimes difficult to determine where grasslands end and the adjacent environment begins. By and large, however, there is a general pattern to grassland types. Although in nature such features as mountains and oceans can obscure the way the forest grades through grassland to desert, the range may be thought of as a spectrum. Starting with the forest at one end, both climate and the environment change in a predictable sequence, the climate shifting from humid to subhumid to semiarid and then to arid. Where the humid climate grades into subhumid, trees are likely to merge with grasslands, forming an open woodland without a closed forest canopy. All such areas, where trees and shrubs are separated by expanses of grass, are defined as savannas by some scientists. Other experts define savannas as grasslands typical of Africa; and they classify this type of area as "woodland savanna."

As aridity increases, trees thin out and shrink to shrub and scrub, eventually disappearing and leaving a landscape covered solely by grass. Grasses may be divided into tallgrass (1.5–3 meters), midgrasses (0.5–1.5 meters), and shortgrasses (0.1–0.5 meters). The taller grasses indicate moist habitats, the short grasses dryer habitats. Of course soil type also plays a role in determining the kind of grass present. Due to these environmental factors the different types of grasslands may have a mosaic pattern of distribution, and in certain areas the boundary between them may be sharp.

All these grassland types occur on various continents. Tallgrass communities, for instance, are found on the prairies of North America, where they may consist of big bluestem (*Andropogon gerardii*) and slough grass (*Spartina michauxiana*), on the llanos and pampas of South America, where the tall *Paspalum fasciculatum* dominates on the llano and *Cortaderia argentea* on the pampa; the savannas and veldt of Africa with red oat grass (*Themeda triandra*) as well as several species of *Hyparrhenia*, *Cymbopogon*, and *Loudetia* on the savannas; and the maidans of tropical Asia, where the dominant herb is also red oat grass.

Quintessential Grassland

In terms of ecology, the undisturbed American prairie was the quintessential grassland. Along its eastern

14. *Squirreltail grass* (Hordeum jubatum) *of the North Temperate Zone is related to barley. It reaches heights of approximately 70 centimeters and is often considered a weed. Like many other grasses, it is suited to areas of low rainfall and porous soil, and it can withstand a considerable range of seasonal climatic extremes.*

16-17. *During the spring, the sandy grassland of Nebraska blazes with annual sunflowers* (Helianthus) *and sand dropseed* (Sporobolus cryptandrus).

marches, where it confronted the forest, it was characterized by grasses such as big bluestem and switch grass (*Panicum virgatum*). Before white settlers brought the plow to the prairies—which, like other tallgrass regions, are among the best farmlands on earth—the prairies were literally a sea of grass.

As one traveled westward over the American prairie the grass community changed. Reflecting the gradual reduction of moisture toward the west, the grasses, like the trees before them, decreased in height. Just as tallgrasses were interspersed with trees to the east, they here mixed with somewhat shorter grasses such as little bluestem (*Andropogon scoparius*). Still in a subhumid zone, this area, often called the midgrass prairie, extends on a north-south axis from southern Canada to Texas and from Illinois west to central Nebraska.

West of the true prairie, the climate becomes semiarid. As one approaches the Rocky Mountains, the "high plains" are encountered. Here is a stark, windswept landscape of immense horizons, searing hot in summer and bleak in winter. Counterparts of the high plains, or, more technically, "shortgrass plains," are the steppes of the Eurasian heartland, the southern Serengeti Plain in Tanzania, and the dry spinifex grasslands rimming the desert in western Australia. Such shortgrass plains tend to merge with desert.

The climate on grasslands can reach extremes. On the Canadian prairies, the winter temperature may drop to minus 46 degrees C.; the summer heat may be almost 80 degrees higher than the winter low.

Temperature ranges are not nearly as great on tropical grasslands. For example, on the African equatorial savanna of the Rutshuru Rwindi Plains, in the Virunga National Park of Zaïre, September, the hottest month, has an average temperature of 23.9 degrees C., only 2.4 degrees above the mean for July, the coolest time of the year. The average daily temperature range in any month, however, can be as much as 16 degrees C., due to cooling winds from nearby mountains, some of which tower more than 5000 meters high.

Wind is another important factor in forming and maintaining grasslands. By promoting evaporation, it reduces the humidity favorable to trees. At the same time, the pounding of the wind also interferes with tree growth, while relatively low-growing grasses, anchored by huge masses of roots, escape the worst of the buffeting.

Climatic changes, especially those affecting precipitation, can have a marked impact upon a grassland, most dramatically in places where one environment borders on another. Where tallgrass meets trees, or mingles with shortgrass, for example, the ecological balance is so delicate that even a seemingly minor modification in climate can change the vegetation in just a generation or two. During the "Dust Bowl" years of the 1930s, for instance, the shortgrass prairies of the United States crept eastward into tallgrass that was less able to prosper in the increasingly dry climate. When the drought ended, the tallgrass regained the ground it had lost.

The conflict between the various zones of vegetation can be purely a local skirmish or it can span a continent. A dramatic example of how the competition can range over

Monarch butterflies (Danaus plexippus) are found all across North America from Mexico to southern Canada. They thrive on prairies, where, as caterpillars, they find many of the plants, such as butterfly weed (Asclepias tuberosa), on which they feed. Like the other plants favored by the monarchs, butterfly weed belongs to the milkweed family (top row, left). Before becoming an adult, the caterpillar spins a silk "button" with which it attaches itself to a branch (center). The caterpillar begins to form a pupa, called a chrysalis, which is surrounded, not by silk as in moths, but by a chitinous coating which hardens into a protective cover (right). While a pupa, the butterfly is gradually transformed into an adult; its limbs and mouth parts change

and it develops wings (bottom row, left). The metallic yellow spots of the monarch's hardened, dried chrysalis are protective as well as beautiful. Because the developing butterfly appears inanimate, the monarch is less attractive to predators (center). A month after beginning life as an egg, the adult monarch emerges from the chrysalis, its wings still moist and wrinkled. As the new adult fans its wings, fluid that has begun circulating through the body is pumped into the wings, expanding them. Meanwhile, the body shrinks to adult proportions (right). The adult monarch will migrate as far south as Mexico in the fall. Several broods of these butterflies may be produced in a single season (bottom).

21 top. *The vast Serengeti Plain of Tanzania is absolutely treeless in some places and dotted with acacia woodland in others. Immense herds—approximately 2 million animals, including antelopes and zebras—migrate across the plain before and following seasonal rains. The concentration of grazing and browsing animals in Serengeti demonstrates the capacity of grasslands to sustain animal life, particularly large mammals.*

Center. *On the North American prairie belt, stands of forest with trees such as oaks* (Quercus) *compete with grasses. A prolonged dry period may encourage the grasses to invade the forest, whereas a shift to damper weather could favor tree growth.*

Bottom. *Kangaroo grass* (Themeda australis) *and eucalyptus trees* (Eucalyptus alba) *grow on the grasslands of New Guinea (as shown here), as well as in nearby Australia. The grasslands of the Australian region are more arid than many similar areas elsewhere in the world.*

Overleaf. *Lions* (Panthera leo) *are at the top of the food pyramid on the African grasslands. They feed on grazing herds and also scavenge the kills of other predators.*

an immense area can be found in Africa during the Pleistocene Epoch. At that time glaciations repeatedly chilled the earth's temperate regions.

While temperate lands were glaciated, the tropics experienced wet stages called "pluvials." In these eras, the equatorial forest of Africa expanded into what had been grasslands during the dry "interpluvials." About 12,000 years ago, after the last pluvial (and the last ice age), the forest retreated once more. It has probably not diminished, however, to the point reached during earlier interpluvials.

Grass and Fire

Grasslands have an ally against forest in the form of fire, started either by lightning or by humans. Although fire destroys both grass and trees, the former regenerates more quickly after a burn. Flames may destroy the grass blades as they do tree trunks, branches, and leaves, but the major portion of the grass is underground, in the form of roots and similar structures.

Fires sweeping through the border country of forest and savanna force the trees to give way to grasses. Conversely, however, burning at the edge of grasslands toward more arid areas promotes the advance of deserts into the more fertile grass country. Thus, fire can be a double-edged sword.

Considerable research on the impact of fire on temperate grasslands has been undertaken. These studies indicate that such grasslands may benefit from the burning of excessive litter—dead plants and other debris. Scientists subjected a few patches of virgin prairie in the midwestern United States to regular burning, and found that tallgrass in the burned places flourished much more markedly than in the control zones. Where fire had swept the prairie, moreover, plants such as asters and goldenrod, competitors of the grasses, were reduced.

Peoples living on tropical grasslands in South America, Asia, and Africa have practiced annual burning of grasses for generations, believing it promotes their growth. In the tropics, however, the disadvantages of fire can outweigh its benefits, especially when deliberate burning is carried on in the dry season, as is often the custom. Flames easily burn out of control on dry tropical grasslands.

All the facts are not in, but there is considerable evidence that the habit of annual burning on tropical grasslands should be abandoned. On the African savanna, for example, the litter of dead grass can be broken up or decomposed by many other forces than fire. Herds of animals trample litter, and it is also consumed by rodents and the termites ever present on African grasslands. Thus decomposed, rather than burned, the litter contributes to the fertility of the soil. In savanna soil, fire also destroys myriad tiny animals. Thus, the raging fires that are set on these grasslands by humans, or ignited by lightning, kill so many different organisms at the lower levels of ecological webs that the entire natural balance is thrown out of kilter.

Nature of the Grasses

Consisting of about 4500 species, the grass family, Gramineae, is the single most important group of plants to

humans. All cereals—such as oats, wheat, and corn—are domesticated grasses. Even sugarcane is a grass, as is rice, and bamboo, a giant of the group.

A grass plant has a stem, leaves, or "blades," and flowers. The flowers are not at all showy: they are not brightly colored, and they have no petals. Clusters of grass flowers often appear as wispy brushes or feathery flags atop the long stems, from which the leaves sprout at intervals. When the flowers release pollen, it rides the wind, dispersing far and wide, and spreading the kingdom of the grasses.

Grasses also reproduce by means of underground runners called rhizomes. In no time at all, a single grass plant can produce enough rhizomes to carpet the area all around it with new plants. While pollen reproduces grasses sparsely over great distances, "vegetative" reproduction by rhizomes consolidates the hold of grasses on the soil in their immediate area.

Rhizomes join two other structures, roots and tillers, to form the dense, tough matting that holds the soil in place. This matting is so solid that early settlers on the American prairie cut it into slabs and used it to build their "sod houses." Underneath the plant are roots, anchoring it down as much as seven feet deep in the ground. From the stem, just at ground level, grow side shoots called tillers, which give the plants a grip on the surface.

The more a grass stem is broken, bruised, or cut, the more tillers the plant produces. Stems also burgeon forth, so that new leaves rapidly replace those which have been removed. For these reasons, a lawn that is regularly mown, or grassland that is frequently but not excessively grazed, generates growth that is healthy and thick.

Grassland Origins

Once, although the world was green, there was no grass. Nor, in fact, did a flower grace any part of the planet, despite the fact that vegetation was lush. True flowering plants, more advanced than conifers, ferns, horsetails, and other earlier groups, did not appear on earth until the great age of reptiles was well underway. The earliest flowering plants arrived millions of years after the first dinosaurs. How long ago they evolved is uncertain, but their known fossils go back 125 million years.

The grasses themselves evolved about 90 million years ago. But not until 25 million years ago, in the epoch known geologically as the Miocene, did they truly come into their own.

The Miocene was a time of cooling temperatures, increasing aridity, and uplifting of continents. These conditions favored grasses, which invaded the thick forests that for millions of years had had uncontested control of the landscape. As the forests gave way, the first great grasslands appeared.

An example of how various climatic and geologic factors combined to promote the growth and spread of grasslands can be found in western North America. During the Miocene, the Rocky Mountains, although long established, uplifted. As their height increased, they blocked the winds blowing east from the Pacific Ocean. The winds dropped their moisture on the western slopes of the mountains. To the east, precipitation became so scant that trees dwindled and grasses slowly dominated.

Top. *The long-billed curlew* (Numenius americanus) *nests on prairies and plains of western North America, usually near marshes or other wetlands.*

Bottom. *A gopher snake* (Pituophis melanoleucus) *prepares to eat the egg of a long-billed curlew. This serpent, which may reach a length of 2 meters, inhabits much of the plains area of North America.*

An Explosion of Mammals

When the grasslands expanded into the forest, a whole new set of niches opened up for mammals, which for about 40 million years had been the dominant land vertebrates. The interface of grasslands and woodland, whether in the Miocene or today, favors an increase in the diversity of animal life. The combination of environments offers a larger variety of food and places to live.

Importantly, natural savannas, steppes, prairies, and other grasslands can support far greater concentrations of mammals—particularly large ones—than forests. The early grasslands were the home of the most immense array of large mammals ever found on earth. When in perfect natural balance, moreover, grassland offers optimal conditions not only for the big mammals but for myriad other forms of terrestrial animal life.

The secret of the ability of grass to support such a large and varied assemblage of animal life is in the ovary of its flower. Once pollinated, the ovary develops as a cereal grain. Packed into the tiny hull of the grain are starches and other foods in which the energy of sunlight has been converted into a form usable by herbivores. More of this energy is available to animals on a grassland than in any other terrestrial environment.

The herbivores that first took advantage of the new food supply are typified by an early horse, known as *Merychippus*. It arose out of ancestors which lived quietly in the forest, where they browsed on leaves and buds. The pony-sized *Merychippus*, however, was not a browser, but had teeth with high crowns, adapted for grinding up the tough grasses of the plains.

The feet of this ancient horse showed another adaptation that helped it open up the grasslands to its tribe. It had three toes, but the middle one was so much larger than the others that it was well on the way to becoming a hoof. The splayed and multi-toed foot of *Merychippus*'s ancestors might have been suitable for scampering over a soft forest floor, but on the hard ground of the grasslands it was a liability. Grasslands provide few places to hide, and survival often depends on the ability to gallop fast and far—something a hoof permits.

While the first horses were leaving the forest for the open country, another group of hoofed mammals, the Bovidae, trod upon the grasslands. They and the grasslands, in fact, originated at the same time, and most bovids still live in grass country. The Bovidae, which includes cattle, antelopes, and gazelles among many others, became remarkably successful as grasslands creatures.

The bovids not only possess a hoof but are also true ruminants: they have stomachs of many chambers and chew cud. They can gulp down food and move on, digesting it later at their leisure, perhaps in a haven away from predators. Bovids also bear young quickly, birth sometimes taking less than an hour. The young are helpless for only a short period; the offspring of many species are on their feet in minutes. This is one of the many adaptations for surviving predation that bovids evolved on the wide-open grasslands.

Bison (*Bison bison*), wildebeest (*Connochaetes taurinus*), and many other bovids gather in large herds which migrate seasonally across the grasslands. Extensive seasonal movements, typified by those of wildebeest herds on the East African savannas, are another adaptation for grasslands life.

Grasslands Layers

The animals of the grasslands utilize virtually all edible vegetation. The same grassland can be the feeding ground for creatures as varied as hippopotamuses, rhinoceroses, African elephants, buffaloes, giraffes, antelopes, warthogs, hares, bustards, various birds of prey, cranes, and innumerable other vertebrates and invertebrates. The large grazing animals use two of the three layers, or strata, of the grasslands environment: the floor (or surface of the soil) and the herbaceous level (the portion of the grasses and other plants above the earth). The third layer is subterranean.

The life of the herbaceous layer and floor is most obvious to the average observer of grasslands. With the grazing animals are multitudes of others, large and small. Many insects, some frogs, and mammals live almost exclusively in the herbaceous layer. The harvest mouse (*Micromys minutus*) of Eurasia, for example, attaches its nest to grass stems.

Many smaller animals use more than one layer. Rabbits, hamsters, guinea pigs, ground squirrels, and other rodents feed on the floor but live underground. Although hidden from our view, the subterranean layer of grasslands teems with life. For example, 47 percent of steppe mammals, as compared with 6 percent of forest mammals, live underground.

All the organisms living above, in, or below the grasses join in a complex web of ecological relationships. The key to the network is the grass itself. Its dense roots, rhizomes, and tillers protect the soil on which the entire system is based. Thick grass cover can reduce the heat of the sun on the ground by as much as 15 degrees C., preventing the earth from hardening into an impervious crust, permitting moisture to soak into the soil, while at the same time shielding it from the impact of rain. The grass mat and the humus it creates filters melting snow and rainwater, giving rise to crystal-clear streams.

If grass cover is reduced to a few inches in height, more than half of the rain will immediately run off, taking soil with it. If grass cover is removed entirely, as it has been in many places by overgrazing, perhaps two thirds of the rain will sluice off the land, carrying away the topsoil and turning rich earth into desert. The water itself flows in muddy, raging torrents, gullying the ground and posing a hazard to life and property.

Once grassland soil has been swept away, it is difficult if not impossible to replace, at least within many human lifetimes. In North America, for example, it takes nature as long as 250 years to replace an inch of topsoil.

Poor agricultural practices in many parts of the world—such as a century ago on the American prairies and today in many developing countries—are ruining grasslands by destroying grass cover and creating barren wastes. A prime offense against grasslands has been the assembling of domestic livestock beyond the carrying capacity of the land. This is made possible by supplying water for the animals, controlling disease, and discouraging predators. Such concentrations of cattle, goats, and sheep destroy

Overleaf. An adult great horned owl (Bubo virginianus) *watches over its young in a nest on the treeless grassland of southeastern Oregon. This owl ranges in North America from the Arctic to the tropics and from coast to coast. Its wide range indicates that it is highly adaptable: in forests it nests in trees, but where no trees are available it rears its young on the ground.*

the grasslands environment by literally eating it up and then trampling what remains, paving the way for erosion.

Under natural conditions, however, the same grassland might support a huge assemblage of wild animals. Behind this seeming contradiction is a system of natural checks and balances. While wild animals seem to reproduce as fast as they can, the numbers of each species presumably are limited by factors such as food supply, predation, disease, and even social structure. The "territorial" behavior of some individual animals, for instance, may cause the death by starvation of others, by excluding them from feeding areas. This natural limit is generally placed on populations. Given balanced environmental conditions, no one species of animal increases beyond what is healthy for the entire system. The vast number of wild animals that grasslands such as those in Africa can support stems from the fact that they provide food for many different types of species. The wide variety of diets of these animals makes it possible for many more of them to share a habitat than if all belonged to only a few groups, eating much the same sort of food. At the same time, the wild animals interact with the environment, promoting its welfare rather than overutilizing it. Many grasslands vertebrates, for instance, help spread plants. A creature may carry seeds or pollen on its coat or control parasites that inhibit plant growth.

The African elephant can have a markedly beneficial impact on its environment, contributing productive changes in vegetation, opening up dense forests by breaking down trees, so that sunlight penetrates to permit the growth of lush, low foliage. Thus a greater variety of food becomes available to plant-eating creatures. The elephant also can aerate the soil when it digs for underground water in dry periods, and thus create drinking sources for other animals.

Additionally, the seasonal migrations of elephants and similar creatures spread the animals and their feeding pressure evenly over a very broad ecosystem. The entire process outlined above generates a giant symbiosis between vegetation and wildlife, which if undisturbed protects and preserves the grasslands.

The mounting human populations and attendant pressure upon grassland by farms, ranches, and other forms of human development have interfered with this natural interplay. Many national parks in Africa, for example, have been carved out of the landscape with little thought of their ecological integrity. Elephants hemmed into such national parks by farms and homesteads cannot travel to new feeding grounds according to age-old patterns. Restricted to a reserve, they eventually destroy their habitat.

Natural grasslands are only a memory in much of the world. In other places, a few scattered remnants survive. Only in a few regions are there large tracts of grassland in undisturbed or relatively natural condition. Even the savannas of East Africa are no longer boundless. Where grasslands remain in a natural state, however, humanity has the opportunity to observe nature at its most bountiful, and perhaps profit by the example. Man still has the possibility of restoring what he has destroyed, but time is short.

Above. *Traveling across the savanna, a herd of African elephants* (Loxodonta africana) *troops along under acacia trees. The elephant feeds on a spectrum of savanna vegetation: it grazes on grasses and browses on trees and shrubs.*

Left. *The body of the giraffe* (Giraffa camelopardalis) *is well suited to savanna life. Its long legs facilitate rapid movement and its great height enables it to see for long distances.*

Overleaf. *A herd of buffaloes* (Syncerus caffer) *rumbles over the Botswana savanna. African buffaloes inhabit both forest and grassland, but the grassland animals are larger than their forest brethren and are darker in color, some are almost black, whereas the forest dwellers are reddish brown. Like many other horned ungulates, the buffalo is gregarious. Its herds are especially large during seasonal migration.*

The Boundless Horizons of Eurasia

Girdling Eurasia is a great swath of grassland stretching from Manchuria in the east to the Ukraine in the west, with an outlier in Hungary. The latter is a remnant of more extensive open country in the glacial times of the Pleistocene Epoch. The immense Eurasian grassland consists of three belts, forming a north-south pattern that is quite distinct, although broken in some places.

In the north is wooded steppe, the outer march of the grasslands kingdom, bordering the boreal birch and evergreen forest in Asia and a broadleaf oak woodland in Europe. Just south of the wooded steppe is a belt of grassy steppe. Next comes a steppe so dry it fades almost imperceptibly into the desert which, especially in Asia, lies at the heart of the continental land mass.

There are, however, significant exceptions to the pattern, some natural, others caused by man. On the Iranian plateau, the grasslands motif is determined largely by altitude instead of latitude. The bleak desert and dry scrub at the center of the plateau is ringed by irregular bands of steppes, wooded at high altitudes and grassy below. A few grasslands grow on the mountainous rim of the great Arabian desert.

India has several mixtures of tropical grasslands, although much of their natural character has been destroyed by human activities. Some are cultivated, others reduced by overuse to desert.

European grasslands, too, have largely vanished, most of them converted to farmland, so the north-south pattern so clear in Asia is obscured in many places. Today, only a few remnants of European steppes remain, almost all in the form of reserves. Once upon a time, the grasslands of Russia and Hungary—the latter known as "puszta"—must have afforded magnificent vistas—grassy seas flecked with flowers in summer, barren in winter, but abounding in animals at any season.

The vast plain of Hungary, where wetlands and tree groves were interspersed with grasses, has largely been taken over by cultivation. But between the Danube and Tisza rivers, something of the original puszta remains. It is a wide treeless grassland that floods in the wet season. The wetlands and shores of the shallow lakes are frequented by white storks (*Ciconia ciconia*), Kentish plovers (*Charadrius alexandrinus*), lapwings (*Vanellus vanellus*), black-tailed godwits (*Limosa limosa*), and avocets (*Recurvirostra avosetta*).

As an isolated outpost of the great Eurasian steppe, the puszta has many mammals which are also found further to the east. These include a number of small rodents, such as European susliks (*Spermophilus citellus*), steppe mice (*Sicista subtilis*), and voles.

The Wooded Steppe, a Meeting Ground

Each belt of steppe has a characteristic plant and animal life, although many species occur in more than one of the zones, and some inhabit both a steppe belt and adjacent woodland or desert. On the Eurasian steppes the range of climatic extremes is much greater than on other grasslands, such as the African savanna, and so extreme pressure is placed on the inhabitants.

While each of the three steppe belts has its own common character, some differences appear in the landscape on either side of the Ural River, the boundary between the

Above. *Two male European hares* (Lepus europaeus) *box and kick as they battle for the right to mate with females.*

Opposite. *The long, powerful hind legs of the hare make it well suited to life on open terrain. It can travel at speeds of up to 70 kilometers an hour.*

grasslands of Europe and Asia. The wooded steppe, for example, is influenced by the type of forest it abuts. Since the European wooded steppe is adjacent to a broadleaf forest, it is dotted with groves of oaks, chiefly English oak (*Quercus robur*). The groves on the wooded steppe in Asia are not primarily oak; instead, birches have invaded the grassland from the boreal forest.

From the northern forest, animals have also come out onto the steppe, both in Europe and in Asia. Among the large mammals are the moose (*Alces alces*) and the roe deer (*Capreolus capreolus*). The breaking up of forests into plantations and farmlands in Siberia and Russia has favored these animals, so they have increased and spread to the wooded steppe.

On the northern steppe, the roe deer in particular appears locally to have taken up part of the role of ungulates that no longer live there. Among those that have become extinct are the European bison (*Bison bonasus*) and the aurochs (*Bos primigenius*), a great wild ox. The bison (still surviving in a few eastern European forest reserves) and the aurochs, which lived mainly in the forests, seasonally moved out onto the wooded steppe and thence to the grassy steppeland.

The roe deer is at home in a variety of temperate habitats, ranging from mountains to steppe. One geographical race or another of this highly adaptable animal lives in a belt across Eurasia from the Atlantic to the Pacific. It is a deer of small to medium size, weighing at most about 50 kilograms. The further east roe deer live, the greater the size of their bodies and antlers seems to be. The Siberian race of the roe deer may be twice as heavy as those of the central European forests.

Immediately prior to the mating period, when the female comes into heat, roe deer perform spectacular rituals. There is repeatedly a kind of lovemaking between the doe and the buck but without actual copulation. The female dances about in front of the male with amazing jumps and short rushes. She often provokes the male to a frantic chase for ten to fifteen minutes or even longer. She leads him in a circular course over the countryside or in smaller circles around a bush or stone. The male follows closely behind her uttering a grunting, hoglike sound. The performance gives the false impression that the male is chasing the female, but in reality she takes the initiative and is master of the play! Then suddenly she stops, and the two stand still, or lie down, a short distance apart. Mating occurs in the weeks that follow, usually without ceremony.

The boreal and broadleaf forests have also contributed carnivores to the wooded steppe, including the stone marten (*Martes foina*) and badger (*Meles meles*). They belong to the same family, the mustelids.

Of the two, the badger is the more far-ranging, occurring from the fringes of the subtropics to the cold northern lands. In northern areas, such as the wooded steppe, it is active from late spring to late autumn. It spends the winter in a den. It does not truly hibernate but sleeps deeply with slightly reduced body metabolism and not so soundly that it cannot wake and take a short walk— without eating—on a mild winter day.

Because it does not feed in winter, the badger eats heavily in late summer and autumn and builds up an impressive

layer of fat that serves as fuel during its cold-weather dormancy. The females particularly need this store of nutrients because a number of physiological changes related to reproduction occur while they are dormant. The badger mates between May and July, although if a female is not fertilized then, she may come into heat again in October. Embryonic development, however, does not begin until January, and one to five young appear by February or March. The interval between mating and development of the embryo is caused by delayed implantation in the uterus, a circumstance not uncommon in the mustelids.

The burrows in which badgers spend the day, and the winter, are often centuries old, becoming larger and more labyrinthine through continuous use by successive generations. Burrows have been found with tunnel systems 310 meters long, from which up to 25 tons of earth have been removed.

Some dens are the home of several badger families. Although territorial, badgers can be social animals. When a large number inhabit the same area, scent, vision, and vocalizations keep them from getting in each other's way.

Like most wooded steppe mammals, the badger is not restricted to the forest and wooded steppe, but also ranges into the more open grasslands.

Because the wooded steppe is a mixture of grass and forest, it accommodates many creatures which can live in either of these habitats. Many songbirds in particular prosper in the mosaic of glades and trees. The small glades hold linnets (*Carduelis cannabina*) and goldfinches (*C. carduelis*) in abundance. Dense thickets shelter thrush nightingales (*Luscinia luscinia*), and these chorus beautifully in the spring and early summer on the European steppes and the adjacent areas of Asia. The melodious fanfares of the thrush nightingale have to be learned by the young birds. They must be able to hear an adult male with a developed song. During the incubation period, lasting about two weeks, the male sings at night and feeds its brooding mate by day. Once the nestlings have hatched, the male is too busy feeding them to sing. As soon as they leave the nest, however, he starts again. Apparently this is when the young learn the song, although they will not use it until sexual maturation a year later. However, it is also possible that the male embryos imprint the song while still in the egg.

Some of the most spectacular birds of the wooded steppe are the species that winter in Africa. Among them are rollers (*Coracias garrulus*), which in flight display a cascade of green, azure blue, olive, chestnut, purple, and black. They are joined by bee-eaters (*Merops apiaster*), with yellow, chestnut, white, and greenish-blue coloration.

Birds of the Grassy Steppe

As a group, the birds of the grassy steppe are markedly different from those living in the mix of trees and glades. Out in the open, among the feather grasses (*Stipa*), fescue (*Festuca*), and bluegrass (*Poa*), live ground birds, one of the most spectacular of which is the demoiselle crane (*Anthropoïdes virgo*). This bird, whose range straddles the Europe-Asia border region, is not large for a crane—

The common vole (Microtus arvalis) *is unusually prolific. Females may breed at an age of 11 to 21 days, males at about 6 weeks. Voles are a prime source of food for predators such as snakes, owls, birds of prey, and flesh-eating mammals.*

it stands about a meter high. Its plumage is elegant, mainly ashy blue-gray, with black on most of the neck and the elongated breast feathers. Large tufts of soft white plumes behind each eye add to its beauty.

The demoiselle cranes arrive on the grassy steppe to breed in March. They gather at certain traditional sites on dry ground and perform an elaborate dancing ritual. The cranes form an irregular circle on a patch of ground that serves as the dance arena. Within the circle, small groups of cranes take turns dancing before the others. As soon as one group finishes its performance, another starts. With wings half spread, the dancers run back and forth, bowing, jumping up and down, or remaining in a half-reclining pose. Sometimes the birds stretch out their necks, spreading the throat feathers and uttering either a guttural or a trumpeting sound.

Among the other ground birds of the grassy steppe are the bustards and partridges. The great bustard (*Otis tarda*) and little bustard (*O. tetrax*) have become rare. Of these species the great bustard is remarkable. It is the largest bird of Europe. The male weighs up to 15–16 kilograms and has a total length of about 110 centimeters. It has a stout body with long thick neck and legs. The female is a dwarf by comparison, weighing only about 6 kilograms. The great bustard is specialized to the steppe, but since natural grasslands have become scarce, it has adapted to cultivated, treeless lands, despite the fact that it is extremely shy. The latter feature is easy to understand since this bird has for centuries been persecuted by man all over its range. The great bustard occurs in flocks which keep together during cold spells but become looser when the weather is favorable. From a distance the large birds may be taken for grazing sheep.

These bustards share their habitats with many small rodents and, like them, are vegetarians, but during their breeding season the birds, and particularly the females, begin to eat insects, frogs, and rodents. The nuptial display of the male is one of the most extraordinary events in the bird world. The mainly buff-colored male turns its plumage almost inside out into a billowy mass of white feathers, transforming itself into something that bears little resemblance to a bird. This bizarre performance is accomplished by the turning over of the wing coverts and tail feathers, so as to display white undersides. The wings are drooped so they almost touch the ground; the tail is turned forward flat on the back, the head is sunk on the shoulders, the moustaches of whitish bristles stand almost upright, the gular sac is greatly inflated, and the legs bend so that the breast is lowered near the ground. In this posture the bird shakes its wings as if they were only loosely attached to the body. The whole bird becomes a conspicuous white flash signal visible far away over the wide expanses. This is probably the purpose of the exercise: to visually herald its presence to far-distant females.

Even more typical of grassy steppes than ground birds are birds of prey, which find the wide-open expanses quite suited to their far-ranging hunting flights. Patrolling over the grasses are the imperial eagle (*Aquila heliaca*), the long-legged buzzard (*Buteo rufinus*), and the pallid harrier (*Circus macrourus*).

Overleaf. *Hoopoes* (Upupa epops) *range from the Atlantic shores of Europe to China. Its name derives from its call, a distinct "poo-poo-poo." The bird's long bill facilitates the capture of insects in the soil and on the ground.*

Above. *The yellow-necked mouse* (Apodemus flavicollis) *favors bushy forests and thickets, where it may nest between the roots of shrubs. It sometimes constructs a nest —made of dry leaves and grass—in the hollows of small trees.*

The harrier flies low, often at only a meter or two above the ground. Sailing tirelessly, on outspread wings that seem never to move, the bird looks for small rodents, its staple diet. Since the rodents go underground for the winter, the harrier migrates to the African savanna, returning only with the warm weather and the reemergence of rodents.

Rodents and Reptiles

Probably the most numerous of the rodents over much of the grassy steppe in Russia is the spotted suslik (*Spermophilus suslicus*), a ground squirrel belonging to a group inhabiting most of the treeless grasslands of Eurasia. The spotted suslik dwells in colonies, but dens individually. The den has a main entrance tunnel up to 6 meters long, with numerous side corridors. The nest chamber in the female's burrow may be more than 2 meters deep.

Several types of reptiles and amphibians inhabit the grassy steppes, where they feed on abundant invertebrate life. The sand lizard (*Lacerta agilis*) and steppe lizard (*Eremias arguta*) are active during the warm months, although in the heat of the summer day they seek the cool recesses of rodent burrows.

Among the snakes, the venomous steppe viper (*Vipera ursinii*) is the species likely to be seen most often by people, mainly because it moves so slowly. It is found from Europe to Mongolia. Less obvious but rather common in many places is the harmless European whip snake (*Coluber jugularis*), which despite its name lives as far east as Iran. Reaching more than 3 meters in length, it is the longest serpent of Europe.

Wherever small ponds or lakes appear on the grassy steppes, amphibians may be found. Common are the green toad (*Bufo viridis*) and edible frog (*Rana esculenta*). The toad shows a key adaptation to steppe life. It needs ponds only temporarily, to spawn and develop through the tadpole stage. After that, as an air-breathing adult, it can range far from water as long as it can keep its skin moist from an internal water supply. Like other small steppe animals, however, it is forced underground by extremes of climate—excessive heat or drought, or winter cold.

The Saiga

Unlike small steppe dwellers, the larger animals, particularly on totally treeless grasslands, can find no shelter from summer heat, winter cold, or other elements of the harsh Eurasian climate. They have adapted to escaping the worst weather by migrating, often over great distances. No other animal has demonstrated this more graphically than the saiga (*Saiga tatarica*), an antelope-like ungulate that once ranged across the grassy and dry steppes from western Russia to eastern Asia but has now disappeared from most of its European habitat.

The saiga is a sandy-colored animal that lives in herds of up to 100,000 individuals. It is striking because of a bulbous snout, which is swollen and trunk-like, particularly in the male. The function of the huge snout is uncertain, although scientists suspect it filters the steppe dust in the dry summer, or in wintertime warms the cold air before it enters the lungs.

Able to exist for long periods without water, the saiga gets moisture from the low grasses and shrubs on which it feeds. It flourishes on even the meager vegetation of very arid plains, as well as on the more moist grassy steppes. Thirteen percent of the plants eaten by the saiga are not consumed by other animals because they are so salty or even poisonous.

The recent history of the saiga has been quite dramatic. By 1930 it had almost been exterminated due to hunting and a series of unusually severe winters. The total Eurasian population dropped from uncounted millions to a few hundred. The enforcement of protective legislation, along with an improvement in environmental conditions and the animal's high reproductive potential, helped the animal come back. By 1960, the population had increased to 2 million, of which about a quarter lives between the Volga and Ural rivers, with the rest in Asia.

Wild Horses and Camels

Just as the saiga is found in both the grassy and the dry steppes, a number of ungulates live in the dry steppes and in the deserts adjacent to them. This is especially true in Asia, where vast areas of arid steppes merge in the south with deserts. Here one finds animals such as the Mongolian goitered gazelle (*Gazella guttorosa*) and the wild ass (*Equus hemionus*).

The dry steppes of central Asia once were the home of another member of the equine tribe, Przewalski's horse (*E. przewalskii*), which roamed an immense area in China, Mongolia, and the U.S.S.R. Przewalski's horse was the last truly wild horse. The last wild herd, containing 27 animals, was seen in 1969 in Mongolia near the Chinese frontier. An expedition in 1979 found no trace of them. Destruction of habitat and competition with livestock for food and water were major factors in its decline. Since it is easily bred in captivity, however, it may be reintroduced on the steppes. There is no mistaking a Przewalski's horse for a domestic breed. It has very much the look of a wild animal. Chunky, with a large head, the horse seems rugged and powerful. Its black tail and mane, which stands upright, contrast with the buckskin-colored body. The hair on its body grows long and exceptionally shaggy during the cold months, enhancing the wild appearance of the animal.

Pictures of horses that probably were the Przewalski breed were painted on the walls of Pleistocene caves. Very likely, the horse was widespread in ancient times, and even into more recent years. By the last century, however, its last stronghold was the steppes of central Asia. By then it was forgotten by zoologists, who did not suspect that it still existed. In 1879, however, the Polish-Russian explorer Nikolai Przewalski discovered the horses in their remote haven.

Few observations of this last wild horse were taken in the wild. In zoos, however, much has been learned of their behavior, and it is assumed their actions in captivity resemble those in the natural state. The male, for instance, often brings up the rear of the herd, keeping the females and young together, and is ever ready to defend them.

The wild population of the Bactrian camel (*Camelus bactrianus*) is limited to the Gobi and Trans-Altai arid

45 top. *The sunny, flower-strewn grasslands of Eurasia attract a variety of butterflies, including this male orange tip* (Anthocharis cardamines) *perched on forget-me-not flowers* (Myosotis).

Bottom. *Adult marbled white butterflies* (Melanargia galathea) *vary in color from yellow to white. The caterpillars feed on grass. Adults feed on plant fluid such as nectar.*

Overleaf. *A small copper butterfly* (Lycaena phlaeas) *alights on a flower. Copper butterflies are fast fliers that favor open country.*

Among the heaviest flying birds, the great bustard (Otis tarda) *weighs about 12 kilograms and stands more than a meter high. Its courtship display is elaborate. As the male parades about the ground before his intended mate, his feathers are transformed into waving plumes.*

steppes in southern Mongolia and Northern China. These camels may have descended from wild animals or from domesticated ancestors returned to the wild state some time ago. As late as the middle of the nineteenth century, wild camels covered Mongolia and Kazakhstan. During the 1920s the species could be found everywhere in the Gobi semi-deserts and dry steppes, but due to competition with domesticated animals for pasture and water during the following decades, it declined rapidly. Domesticated camels of this species have a much wider range, occurring in steppes and semi-deserts from Asia Minor and the Crimea in the west to China in the east.

Moles, Jerboas, and Polecats

Throughout the dry steppes the mammals that seem to be most numerous and occur in the greatest variety are rodents. Many rodents of the dry steppes are closely related to those of the grassy steppes. On the dry steppes of Mongolia, the yellow steppe vole (*Lagurus luteus*) replaces its grassy steppe short-tailed relative (*L. lagurus*). The spotted suslik disappears, while the pygmy (*Spermophilus pygmaeus*) and yellow (*S. fulvus*) thrive. They spend up to nine months underground, an adaptation not only to cold winter weather but to the very dry autumn.

Dry steppes are the favorite habitat of jumping rodents called jerboas, which are also found in the desert. Twenty of the world's 25 species of jerboas inhabit the arid steppes, especially in Asia. These include the Siberian jerboa (*Allactaga sibirica*) and the great jerboa (*A. major*). The hind legs of jerboas are four times longer than the front legs. Normally, they move about in small hops and on all fours. When frightened, however, they leap prodigiously on their two hind limbs, sometimes for distances of more than three meters.

The dry steppe rodents are preyed upon by both birds of prey and small carnivores. Typical of the birds of prey is the steppe eagle (*Aquila rapax*), also known as the tawny eagle. A ground nester—it has no choice on the treeless steppes—it flies low like the pallid harrier, hunting for susliks and voles. Oddly, however, in its winter home on the African savanna, it often soars high in the air.

The marbled polecat (*Vormela peregusna*), ranging from Russia to Mongolia, is a characteristic small steppe carnivore. It has thick fur, especially in winter, when it must brave fierce winds and cold. Like other small weasels it can wiggle into rodent burrows to find prey. It lives in burrows of its own making, although sometimes it rests in those of other creatures. Two other polecats also inhabit the Eurasian grasslands. One is the European polecat (*Mustela putorius*), the other the steppe polecat (*M. eversmanni*). They are more closely related to the black-footed ferret (*M. nigripes*) of North America than to the marbled polecat.

Polecats are tough, wiry animals, with the agility and persistence typical of all the weasels. The female defends her litter savagely. The long, sharp fangs of these small animals—smaller than domestic housecats—make them adversaries to be feared much more than their size indicates.

Polecats have anal glands capable of producing a powerful noxious scent. When Europeans arrived in the Americas

Dazzling courtship rituals are also typical of the ruff (Philomachus pugnax.) The ruff's name derives from the male's huge collar of feathers, prominent during display. Shore birds that breed on the Eurasian tundra or on some grassland marshes, ruffs are also seen along the coasts as they migrate south for the winter.

and discovered the skunk and its ability to release a strong odor, they were reminded of the polecat, and thus early American pioneers bestowed this name upon the skunk.

Steppes and Savannas of India

A totally distinct Asian steppeland exists—at least in name—on the Indo-Gangetic plain, a crescent-shaped lowland in Pakistan and northern India. This area also has tropical savanna. Due to high population density and intensive cultivation, however, the grasslands have been changed. If the overgrazing and poor agricultural practices carried on in the region would cease, the grasslands would reappear.

Large parts of western India and the non-desert areas of Pakistan are occupied by dry steppe vegetation—sparse grass and an open thorn scrub consisting mainly of acacias, which grow to the size of trees. These give the landscape the look of a woodland steppe. Indians call this kind of woodland—the area's climax vegetation—a "thorn forest." It is a hot area, with temperatures reaching about 40 degrees C. The annual average temperature is 25 degrees C. and the annual precipitation ranges between 480 and 760 millimeters but may drop as low as 250 millimeters.

Within the thorn scrub zone, in the state of Gujarat, lies the Gir Wildlife Sanctuary, home of the last wild Asiatic lions. Of the same species as the African lion, but a different race, the Asiatic lion (*Panthera leo persica*) once ranged from the Middle East to most of the Indian subcontinent. It was primarily a creature of the wide-open savanna, but has retreated into a scrubby grassland, the only place left to it.

In addition to the Asiatic lion the Gir reserve shelters three other powerful predators—the striped hyena (*Hyaena hyaena*), the leopard (*Panthera pardus*), and the sloth bear (*Melursus ursinus*). Besides the enormous number of domestic livestock (buffaloes, cattle, sheep, and goats), there are several species of wild herbivores on which the lion prefers to prey: the huge nilgai (*Boselaphus tragocamelus*), four-horned antelope (*Tetracerus quadricornis*), blackbuck (*Antilope cervicapra*), sambar (*Cervus unicolor*), axis deer (*C. axis*) and the wild boar (*Sus scrofa*), the lion's favorite food.

Until recently the blackbuck was one of the most common and characteristic animals of grasslands in India and Pakistan, but hunters have brought it to the verge of extinction. This species has been introduced on game ranches and reserves in the United States, Mexico, and Argentina, where it has become numerous. In fact, there are more blackbucks in Texas and Argentina than in India and Pakistan.

Blackbuck breeding herds consist of a dominant male and several females. The buck marks its territory with a secretion—produced by scent glands on the head—on stems of grass and twigs of bushes. The buck also delineates its territory by depositing feces around it. When fleeing, the blackbuck leaps high into the air, a habit it shares with several African antelopes.

One of the largest grassland and thorn scrub mammals of India is the nilgai, which weighs up to 275 kilograms. It shares some mating patterns with the blackbuck. At

Opposite. *Palm squirrels* (Funambulus pennanti) *of southern Asian grasslands seek nuts, seeds, plant stems, leaves, insects, and other food by day. The female builds a nest of plant fibers in a tree for her young.*

Overleaf. *A family of bonnet macaques* (Macaca radiata) *of southern Indian scrublands engages in mutual grooming. This activity not only rids them of skin parasites but also builds behavioral bonds. Mothers with infants often are the focus of grooming sessions. Other adult monkeys and juveniles groom the mother and baby, acquainting the infant with the various members of its troop.*

certain times of the year nilgai males occupy and defend a small piece of ground, where they repel other males but gladly accept visiting females and try to retain them within the area. Nilgais both graze and browse, making efficient use of thorn scrub vegetation.

With nilgai and blackbuck in decline, today the most common antelope on the Indian savannas is the Indian gazelle, a race of a species occupying dry grasslands and semi-deserts from northern Africa eastward across Asia. It has been able to adapt to devastated habitats but hunters hold its numbers down.

The Indian hare (*Lepus nigricollis*) and the palm squirrel (*Funambulus pennanti*) are also common on the grasslands; and in the drier areas the Indian gerbil (*Gerbillus gleadowi*) occurs. The largest rodent in the area is the nocturnal Indian porcupine (*Hystrix indica*).

Grassy Valleys and Maidans of Southern Asia

Large areas of southern Asia, particularly in India but also in several southeastern Asian countries, consist of small grasslands surrounded by deciduous forests, monsoon forests, or rain forests. Most of these grasslands are lusher than those of the open plains. Sometimes grasslands encircle swampy areas, with forest nearby. Some grassy valleys penetrate deep into lowland forests; others break into the mountains. This diversity of habitats allows animals to alternate between the various habitats on a daily or seasonal basis. Hence, forest species graze the enclosed grasslands or hunt the animals that forage there. But the enclosed grassy glades and valleys, called maidans in India, also have their own fauna. Among larger mammals supported by this type of habitat are the swamp deer or barasingha (*Cervus duvauceli*), hog deer (*C. porcinus*), and the axis deer or chital.

The barasingha is an extremely handsome animal with an amber brown, lightly spotted coat and graceful, well-proportioned antlers that may be more than a meter long. These deer generally live in open pastures and especially in swamps. They are well adapted to living in swampy areas: their thick hair repels water and their toes spread far apart, whick makes walking on muddy ground easier. Indeed, barasinghas often actually stand in swamp water. The animals feed on swamp vegetation when it is available, but they will eat other plants as well.

Barasinghas of both sexes herd together in the winter; in spring and summer the males go off singly and the females live together in small groups.

Axis deer resemble barasinghas but are more heavily spotted. Unlike other deer, axis deer retain their spots throughout their lifetime and in all seasons. Axis deer are commonly found near rivers and if threatened will often flee into the water. Hog deer in turn resemble axis deer and are closely related to them, but they are much stockier.

The Asiatic Elephant

The Asiatic elephant (*Elephas maximus*) was originally believed to be of the open savanna, but now lives in areas with more trees. The Asiatic elephant differs in many ways from its African relative. It is smaller. While an African bull may reach a height of up to 3.70–4.01 meters, an Indian male elephant seldom attains 3–3.10

meters. The record height is 3.25 meters. An Asiatic elephant weighs about 3.5–5 tons, the African up to 6–7 tons. The two species also have differences in build which are clearly visible from their body silhouettes. The head and particularly the ears are much smaller in the Asiatic elephant and so are the tusks. Moreover, only the bulls of the Indian species have visible tusks, while in the African elephant both sexes have large tusks. In Asiatic elephant females the tusks scarcely extend beyond the lips. The Asiatic elephant is ecologically much less adaptable than its African counterpart. Couples are solitary or are associated with small herds of 15 to 30 individuals, including females, calves, and young males, often under the leadership of a dominant male. Among African elephants, old females are leaders of herds. The Asiatic elephant is easier to tame than the African one. Its association with man goes back thousands of years and is reflected in an even more remote mythology. It was probably domesticated as a riding animal by 2500 B.C. and for several thousand years played a great role as a war animal.

Many of my field trips in tropical Asia have been in the form of comfortable rides on an elephant's back. No amphibious vehicle can compete with elephants as far as pushing through obstacles and maneuverability are concerned. They force their way through almost impenetrable vegetation, and climb or descend steep slopes or cross torrential rivers or muddy marshes. They are highly intelligent and one feels secure in their company when difficult situations arise.

One night in the Kaziranga marshes and grasslands we traveled with four pack elephants in single file. Suddenly the leading male elephant met, head to head, with three Indian rhinos (*Rhinoceros unicornis*). The elephant stopped, spread its ears and moved its trunk in various directions to localize or perhaps count the rhinos. All the rhinos stood motionless with raised heads. After several minutes of silent watchfulness the elephant trumpeted wildly, while the other three elephants moved up beside us, grouping themselves in lined formation about fifteen to twenty meters from the rhinos. The latter became increasingly nervous, snorting and splashing with their feet and taking a few steps back and forth, but they did not move away. I suggested to the mahout on my elephant that we should retreat and leave the rhinos in peace. I do not know whether he misunderstood me, because, instead, he encouraged the elephant to rush toward the rhinos, who immediately fled. Our elephant pursued one of them, but suddenly the rhino turned and charged. The elephant stopped abruptly, rolling up its sensitive trunk like a giant curl between its large tusks as protection. At the same moment the rhino also stopped—only about 2 meters in front of the elephant. Then the mahout intervened, shouting loudly. I do not know whether he intended to scare the rhino or to encourage the elephant. In any event, the elephant changed its tactics. Stamping with its forelegs against the soft, moist ground, thus producing an impressive sound, and shaking its enormous head vigorously sidewise, it advanced courageously against its adversary. The rhino gave up, turned, and disappeared quickly in the tall grass and darkness of the night. That was the end of the duel.

Overleaf. *The Indian barasingha* (Cervus duvauceli) *prefers open marshy areas and grassy maidans. It is a large deer, with antlers more than a meter long. The barasingha often stands in the water for long periods while feeding. Its avoidance of forest in favor of open landscape has made it easy prey for human hunters.*

The axis deer (Cervus axis) *inhabits Indian grasslands and light woodland. These animals breed throughout the year, and males may shed antlers during any season.*

55

Above. *The Indian cobra* (Naja naja), *whose habitats include grassy areas, ranges across the continent's southern tier. It feeds largely on rodents and frogs, often hunting the former in and around homes and on farmlands and the latter in rice paddies. Thus it comes into contact with humans, and probably bites more people than any other venomous snake. It is not, however, unusually aggressive.*

Left. *The king cobra* (Ophiophagus hannah) *of southern Asia is the longest venomous snake, reaching lengths of almost 6 meters. It preys chiefly on other serpents, which it kills and quickly swallows.*

Overleaf. *A golden jackal* (Canis aureus) *stops for a moment on its trek through an Indian grassland. Jackals are key scavengers of tropical grasslands, feeding on kills of larger beasts.*

Africa: Great Herds and Sleek Hunters

Stretching across the landscape in north-central Tanzania in eastern Africa is the Serengeti Plain, an immense savanna largely enclosed in a national park. Here rove large herds of antelope—gazelles and wildebeests, roans (*Hippotragus equinus*), oribis (*Ourebia ourebi*), impalas (*Aepyceros melampus*), elands (*Taurotragus oryx*), and topis (*Damaliscus korrigum*). Zebras thrive. Buffaloes, black rhinos (*Diceros bicornis*), and giraffes are abundant. These plant-eating animals are pursued by carnivorous predators, such as lions (*Panthera leo*), leopards, hyenas, and the fierce African wild dogs (*Lycaon pictus*).

Serengeti, with literally millions of large mammals, is a remnant of what virtually all African grasslands were a century ago, before expanding human populations changed many of them into wastelands. In their natural state the grasslands of Africa are the richest in wildlife of any grassland on earth. The large mammals, in particular, make these grasslands perhaps the most spectacular of all wildlife scenes. Nowhere else do we find so many big herbivores, sometimes in herds of hundreds of thousands. On some African savannas, 30 species of large herbivores and the carnivores that prey on them share the same environment. When smaller carnivores and herbivorous animals are added, the number of species may reach 50, without counting many little mammals such as rodents.

This most remarkable mammalian fauna may be explained by an interplay of several factors, the most important of which is vegetation. The vast range of grassland habitats in Africa includes many vegetation types. Changes in climatic patterns have altered the landscape, leading to temporary or permanent dislocations of plants and animals, but therefore favoring the evolution of many different species.

The great variation in vegetation has led to the development of several types of grassland, often appearing in more than one region throughout the continent. As a rule, the same sort of grassland belts lie at roughly similar latitudes both above and below the equator.

Most African grasslands come under the broad classification of savanna, although of many different types. The driest of these is semi-desert. A major belt of this type lies just south of the Sahara Desert and merges with the desert. It is the Sahel, stretching from the Atlantic across the continent to the Red Sea. The Sahel is mirrored south of the equator by the Karoo of southern Africa and the semi-deserts around the barren heartland of the Etosha Pan National Park in South-West Africa. In such areas, perennial and annual grasses virtually disappear during the long dry season but reappear during the rains.

Another type of dry savanna, generally adjacent to the semi-desert savanna, occurs in the Sudan in the north and in parts of Somalia and northern Kenya in the east, and in South-West Africa and Botswana, for example, the Kalahari in the southern part of the continent. It is a mixture of tall and short grasses along with tough thorny trees and shrubs.

Prominent among the trees of the dry savannas are acacias. In southern Africa, *Acacia giraffae* and *A. haematoxylon* form arid parkland. In the north, one sees

62. *Warthogs* (Phacochoerus aethiopicus) *are found on grasslands throughout most of Africa. Their huge tusks are used for digging up roots and other food and for defense.*

Above. *While common zebras*
(Equus burchelli) *look on, two*
wildebeest (Chonnochaetes
taurinus) *joust on Etosha Pan in*
South-West Africa. Male
wildebeest—also called gnus—
are highly territorial during the
breeding season. When males
contest territory, they often
engage in ritualized combat on
their knees. The winner may be
able to expand his territory.

Left. *On the flat plains of*
Amboseli National Park in
Kenya, a herd of common zebras
stands in the evening light.
Zebras feed primarily at night.
The sound of their eating is
audible and sometimes enables
predators to track them. Lions
are a major predator of zebras.

Right. *Demonstrating the variety of hoofed animals that share the African grasslands, a zebra, a giraffe* (Giraffa camelopardalis), *and a roan antelope* (Hippotragus equinus) *meet at a water hole. One reason that African grasslands can support so many grazing and browsing animals is "competitive exclusion," which means that various species do not seriously compete because their food preferences differ. The giraffe, for example, feeds on leaves toward the top of the tall trees that dot the savanna. Roan antelopes eat grasses on the ground. Zebras consume grasses that are tougher and coarser than those preferred by other grazers.*

Opposite. *There are several geographical races of giraffes, differing according to the shade and shape of their markings. The reticulated giraffe of northeastern Africa is deep chestnut with a pattern of white lines that creates very large patches of a distinctively geometrical shape.*

Overleaf. *Giraffes lope across the plains. When running, these animals often lift one pair of feet at a time.*

many large *A. tortilis*, a tree also widely distributed in Africa south of the equator. The latter has an important ecological role because of its resistance to drought and its relationship to some antelopes, notably gazelles. Acacia seed pods are often attacked by a parasitic worm that eats into the fruit. Before the worm reaches and damages the seeds, the fruit ripens and drops to the ground, where gazelles, and sometimes impalas, immediately consume it. The antelope digestive process kills the worm but allows the seeds to pass unharmed through the intestinal tract. As soon as the seeds fall on soil, they germinate. Thus, the antelopes are fed by the tree while in turn the antelopes promote the tree's reproduction as well as its dispersal.

The herbivores that do best on dry savannas are those which browse as well as graze. Such are the elephants, which can consume shrubs as well as grass. The grazers subsist primarily on grass, which does not grow lush during most of the year on the dry plains.

Where there is a relatively good supply of moisture, the savanna becomes more grassy, constituting another vegetation belt. Here grasses grow a meter high, and although shrubs and trees are scattered they are nevertheless fairly abundant. Grassy savannas stretch across the continent south of the Sahel, north of the equator, and east to the White Nile. Grassy savannas are also found in Zaïre and eastern Africa, and in the south, as in South Africa and Mozambique.

In many parts of Africa, especially on the margins of the great equatorial forest of the Zaïre River basin, trees increase to the point where the savanna becomes wooded. Typical are the so-called Guinean savannas, running from west Africa to northeastern Zaïre. In the south, a vast region with this type of environment is called "miombo," an African term for a habitat in which trees such as *Brachystegia*, *Julbernardia*, and *Isoberlinia* predominate. It stretches from western Angola to the Indian Ocean. Miombo woodland savannas form the largest continuous biome in Africa.

Antelopes, Adaptable and Specialized

From the Sahel to southern Africa, wherever the environment has not been completely disturbed, the cast of hoofed mammals living on grasslands changes only slightly with geography. Many antelopes, moreover, can live in more than one type of habitat as well as over a wide geographical range. The bushbuck (*Tragelaphus scriptus*), for example, can survive in most of subsaharan Africa, in forest, woodland, or grassland, except for truly arid areas.

Other antelopes are more specialized as to habitat, if not geography. One such is the lechwe (*Kobus leche*). It lives almost exclusively in floodplains such as the watery flats of the Kafue River in Zambia. One may see herds of thousands of lechwes spread out over the open plain, where they feed on grass. They also wade into the water to graze on inundated grasses.

Another antelope that likes flooded grasslands is the sitatunga (*Tragelaphus spekei*), one of the most elusive of the larger antelopes of Africa. They are usually solitary but I once came upon a group of fifteen. In areas where sitatungas are undisturbed they graze the savanna or

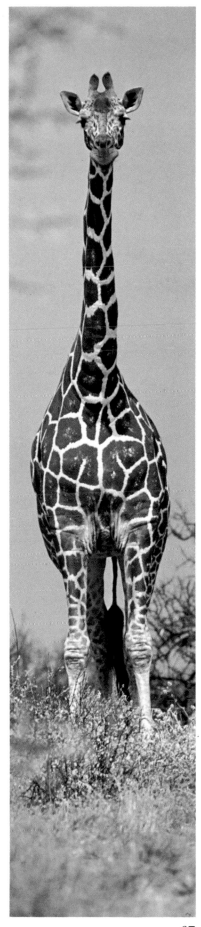

browse the bush by day, but otherwise they are strictly nocturnal. Although it feeds on land, this antelope is well adapted to swamps, where it hides by day. It has greatly elongated hooves which spread out like small snowshoes when it walks on floating swamp vegetation or on mud. It indeed needs this special support in its flooded grassland habitat, because it may weigh over 100 kilograms.

The Kob

A fairly widespread antelope is the kob (*Adenota kob*). It is found across the northern grasslands tier and south of the equatorial forest as well. A large animal, the male weighs up to 90 kilograms. It has a well-proportioned, graceful body gorgeously colored in a glossy, rich red-brown. The adult male has thick horns that bend slightly backward in a double curve.

This animal has a remarkable resistance to heat. It rarely seeks shade, even during the hottest hours of the day, but grazes in the open among grass stems where the soil temperature is about 60 degrees C. Kobs can run very fast, a very useful ability because in certain areas they are the lion's favorite food.

In the Semliki Plain of Uganda and the Kasenyi Plain of Zaïre, male kobs are territorial, keeping mini-territories which have been trampled for decades and perhaps centuries. These well-guarded sites are circular, 30–50 meters across, and lie close to each other. In some parts of the savanna, scores of mini-territories form a collective territory about 300–500 meters wide. Up to thirteen such super-territories have been identified within a limited savanna area. Females wander in herds around the super-territories, but when one wishes to mate she goes alone to a male's mini-territory, where the couple engages in ritualized foreplay before mating.

Close by, on the plains south of Lake Edward in Zaïre, the large kob population is not territorial. The difference in behavior may be due to the fact that these plains are more spacious than the Semliki and Kasenyi plains.

The Sociable Zebras

Often associated with antelope herds are zebras. There are three species, Grevy's (*Equus grevyi*), Burchell's (*E. burchelli*), and the mountain zebra (*E. zebra*). Grevy's is rare, inhabiting only scattered areas in eastern Africa. The mountain zebra, equally uncommon, is found in a few locations in southern Africa, mainly in the Kaokoland highlands of southwestern Africa. Burchell's zebra is divided into several subspecies. It is common and widespread, ranging in eastern Africa from the Sudan to South Africa. Among the subspecies are the Grant's and Chapman's. The nominate Burchell's race itself, ironically, may be extinct.

Zebras are very sociable, always living in groups of five to fifteen animals that may seasonally assemble in large herds. Serengeti zebras usually associate with wildebeest, but they may also forage with giraffes, elands, hartebeest (*Alcelaphus buselaphus*) and other antelopes. Zebras have an extraordinary resistance to the effects of drought: they can eat dry grass and survive easily where cattle die of starvation. Their main natural enemy is the lion. It has been suggested that the stripes of the zebra in a herd may

Above. *The giraffe is the world's tallest living animal, reaching a height of almost 5 meters. The oxpeckers (Buphagus africanus) on the giraffe's neck and back are birds that have a symbiotic relationship with many hoofed mammals. Oxpeckers pick parasites from the skin of the larger beasts; the mammals benefit by being cleaned, the birds by feeding.*

Opposite. *African elephants (Loxodonta africana) spend much of the day feeding. They forage from about three hours before sunrise until late morning. During the midday heat, they rest, but when the afternoon cools, they resume feeding and continue until midnight.*

serve as camouflage, breaking up the body's contours so that it is less visible. However, it is chiefly by night that zebras are preyed upon; at that time predators can easily find them because of the noise they make as they eat.

Great Migrations

Many of the African hoofed animals engage in great seasonal migrations over the plains. In eastern Africa, where a million wildebeest trek back and forth across the Serengeti with the comings and goings of dry and wet seasons, the migration is dramatic. On the savannas north of the equator, the seasonal movements of hoofed creatures may be less visible, involving less spectacular congregations than on the plains of eastern Africa. The antelopes spend much time foraging, so a visitor may not realize that the animals are actually shifting pastures. During migration, red-fronted gazelles (*Gazella rufifrons*), defassa waterbucks, (*Kobus defassa*), roans, giant elands (*Taurotragus derbianus*), and hartebeest usually occur in herds while most other antelopes form smaller groups or remain alone. Topis may gather in herds of several thousand, often mingling with hartebeest and occasionally with kobs and buffaloes.

The Buffalo, Hippopotamus, and Rhino

Living in many of the same habitats as grassland antelopes—although it also roves forest—is the big African buffalo. Savanna buffaloes are larger than their forest kin, with bulls weighing more than 800 kilograms. The buffalo has a reputation among hunters of being Africa's most dangerous animal.

However, wherever I have come close to buffaloes in Africa, they have never shown any sign of aggressiveness. In Zaïre's Virunga National Park, where I spent several years in the field constantly surrounded by buffaloes, they were solitary, in small groups, or in herds of up to 362 animals, the largest assemblage I met. I could approach them to within ten to fifteen meters—and once just three meters—without causing any disturbance. However, wounded buffaloes are terrible adversaries and will often charge a hunter.

The hippopotamus plays a key role in the ecology of the savannas around Lake Edward, where the population of this animal is the largest in Africa. At night, hippos graze on the plains, feeding on *Panicum repens*, a rather short grass that seems to withstand such nightly grazing. The hippos invariably follow the same paths between the lake shores and the plains and so avoid extensive damage. Each hippo consumes 40 to 60 kilograms of grass over a 24-hour period.

The animals spend their days in lakes and in surrounding rivers, where their excreta fertilize algae. These algae, with their attendant zooplankton, are eaten by several species of fishes called breams (*Tilapia*). The breams are very numerous in Lake Edward, where they spawn several times a year and provide predatory fish with food. They are also the basis for a flourishing fishery industry. Over long periods of time, hippos have covered great stretches of the shore of Lake Edward with thick beds of semi-liquid manure. Algae and other microscopic plants important to fish flourish here, along with many organisms which feed great numbers of birds around the lake.

Top. *Female elephants may have four or five infants during a lifetime of perhaps 50 to 60 years. Under healthful conditions, an elephant reaches puberty at between 10 and 12 years, and reaches its full size by about 25. Calves are born after a gestation of about 22 months.*

Bottom. *A young white rhinoceros* (Ceratotherium simum) *rests on the savanna beside its mother. This species is sometimes called the square-lipped rhino because of the shape of its wide mouth, which facilitates the eating of grass. The white rhino is much more of a grazer than the African black rhino* (Diceros bicornis), *which browses on leaves, twigs, and buds.*

Top. *More than a meter long, the ground hornbill* (Bucorvus leadbeateri) *is the largest of the several African hornbills. The male has naked red skin on his throat, whereas the female's throat may be mainly red or blue. During courtship the male's throat swells.*

Center. *Standing on the savanna, a red-billed hornbill* (Tockus erythrorhynchus) *sings its monotonous song of "wot, wot, wot, wot." In dry bush country, such as that of southeastern Kenya, the call of this common bird can be heard throughout the day.*

Bottom. *The yellow-billed hornbill* (Tockus flavirostris) *is another common species of dry bush. Most hornbills have rather extraordinary nesting behavior; the female incubates her eggs in the hollow of a tree—after sealing off the opening except for a small slit, through which the male feeds her. Hornbills feed on a variety of fruits and animals, including snakes.*

Hence, the hippo is a key species in this tremendously productive biocommunity, linking terrestrial grasses with aquatic organisms.

This example illustrates the complexity of an ecosystem comprising savannas, rivers, and a lake, or, more precisely, a flow of energy in a sequence consisting of grass, a mammal, excreta, bacteria, aquatic vegetation, zooplankton, fish, predatory fish, birds, and mammals, including man. The grasses and the dense hippo population make possible the enormous productivity of Lake Edward and the human fishery there. Man has made this unique situation possible by 55 years of strict protection of the Virunga National Park and its ecosystems. This has enabled the hippo population to develop undisturbed, and again shows how wise it is to cooperate with nature and let ecosystems function naturally.

Other savanna animals impressive for their bulk are the rhinoceroses. Both the black (*Diceros bicornis*) and the white (*Ceratotherium simum*) species are increasingly rare in most places. The white rhino breeds successfully in South African reserves, where it has become so numerous that many of the animals have been introduced in areas where they existed before or shipped to dozens of zoos. When the two species coexist in the wild—almost a thing of the past because of their rarity—they do not compete. The black rhino is a browser, eating leaves, twigs, and branches of bushes and small trees, while the white or square-lipped rhino is a grazer, consuming grasses. The two species resemble each other, but the black has a narrow muzzle with a protruding, slightly hooked upper lip, which functions almost as a miniature trunk in seizing leaves and thorny twigs. The square-lipped rhino has a wide mouth adapted for grazing. In temperament the two rhinos are completely different. The black usually prepares to charge as soon as it is disturbed, but this aggressiveness is conditioned by the experience of its previous human contacts. In the few areas where the black rhino has been left in peace it can be most docile. The square-lipped rhino is in general quiet, fearless, and often willing to allow people to approach it. Its lack of shyness has contributed to its rapid decline all over Africa. These two rhinos illustrate how closely related species can avoid competition by feeding on different vegetation.

The Ways of the Elephant

Grandest of the animals seen on the grasslands is the elephant. On the savannas elephants stalk slowly among acacia thickets and red oat grass. They seem without fear, for, as adults, their only enemies are humans.

On the plains of eastern Kivu in Zaïre, elephants can be seen almost constantly. Here we can observe just how they spend their days. About three hours before sunrise the herd begins foraging. The elephants browse and graze until about 10 or 11 A.M. It is by then very hot, so the animals seek shade, and stand quietly, doze or sleep, or else they move into a marsh, lake, or river to drink, wallow, or shower themselves. After a midday siesta, they feed almost continuously until midnight.

The impact of the elephants on vegetation may be profound. Except for man there is no other animal in

Above. *The crowned crane* (Balearica regulorum) *stalks open plains through much of subsaharan Africa, hunting locusts and other small creatures. Cranes also eat vegetable matter. These birds often travel in pairs or even flocks, and especially favor savanna areas around streams, marshes, and water holes.*

Opposite. *All cranes nest on the ground, where they usually lay two eggs, although sometimes the clutch may number only one or as many as three. The eggs of the crowned crane are greenish or blueish; the eggs of other cranes are dull white and brown.*

Africa that can alter a habitat or a landscape so drastically. There are examples of this process in areas where the elephants have been trapped or closed in because of the occupation or destruction of the surrounding areas by man. Both solitary elephants and herds usually keep to a particular area. We observed one elephant which stayed in the same parts of the savanna for weeks. Other herds seemed more nomadic and moved large distances over the plains and into nearby forests in both the lowland and the mountains. Sometimes herds of up to 200 elephants marched in a more or less single file over the savanna.

Large herds consist of cows of all ages and young elephants ranging from the newborn to 14-year-olds. Such a herd is led by an old female with long experience. She has a great responsibility. If she is killed, the herd becomes paralyzed and helpless. Family relationships are of major importance. Young orphans are cared for by females, who invariably show pronounced maternal instincts. Smaller herds are formed by bulls at least 15 years old, but these groups are rather loose and stay together only temporarily. Solitary elephants are almost always bulls. They seek female company only when the females are in heat.

The birthrate of African elephants is related to changing environmental conditions. When food is scarce, the birthrate decreases. In such periods puberty in females is reached between 10 and 20 years of age instead of at 10 years. Moreover, females stop reproducing at the age of 50 instead of at 60 and the interval between births increases to 8 or 9 years instead of 3 or 4 years. The periodicity between peaks and lows is 6–8 years. Similar fluctuations are known in other mammals in both tropical and temperate regions.

During the last decades the populations of the African elephant have been greatly reduced through destruction of its habitat by man and the hunt for ivory. The question now is how long can these remarkably intelligent animals continue to coexist with man?

Warthogs and Porcupines

At the other end of the scale from the elephant are some of the smaller non-carnivorous mammals of the savanna. One that seems to be found everywhere is the warthog. Among African pigs, the warthog is the only entirely diurnal species, grazing on shortgrass and digging for roots, bulbs, and other underground parts of plants. When grazing, it often walks on its foreleg "knees," which are actually its wrists. It frequently makes use of dens dug out by aardvarks, spending an occasional night or longer period in them. Warthogs enter these dens backward to avoid surprise attacks from behind.

If a warthog is cornered, its tusks can serve as good defense weapons, but it usually flees enemies. Warthogs live in families and a couple may be accompanied by the young of its last two litters. The piglets are very vulnerable to carnivores, eagles, and pythons. If young are attacked and cannot escape by running away, the parents will fight even a lion, a leopard, a pack of hyenas, or wild dogs to protect them.

Rodents abound. About 30 species of rodents, and shrews, for example, inhabit the floodplains of Zambia and

adjacent Zaïre. Among them are giant rats (*Cricetomys gambianus,*) and cane rats (*Thryonomys gregorianus* and *T. swinderianus*), which are as large as small pigs. The largest rodent on the continent is the crested porcupine (*Hystrix*). By night it explores the ground for food. When surprised it quickly runs away, its long quills rattling. If charged by a predator, it erects its quills and attacks by moving backward with its mass of quill-spears pointing toward the enemy. When the quills are embedded in the flesh of a foe, they become detached from the porcupine; the muscular movements of the victim seems to force them in deeper and deeper, and they may eventually kill even a large cat.

The Big Cats

Wherever there are herbivores, rodents, and similar animals on the grasslands, there are also the creatures that hunt them, chiefly carnivorous mammals such as cats. One of these is the caracal (*Felis caracal*), a medium-sized cat living on the drier northern, eastern, and southern savannas. A hunting caracal bounds on or rushes lizards, rodents, and shrews, and can jump high in the air from a motionless position to catch low-flying birds. Birds appear to be a common prey for these acrobatic cats. I have seen them catching birds at dusk in such widely separated countries as Upper Volta, Sudan, Somalia, Zaire, Zambia, and South Africa. Caracals also prey on hares (*Lepus capensis* and *L. crawshayi*), which are abundant on most African grasslands but are hardly ever seen because of their strictly nocturnal habits.

Most famous of all the African cats, of course, is the lion. It is unusual in that it is very social, an uncommon characteristic among felines.

The community structure of lions varies; they live in groups called prides, which may contain up to 45 individuals. However, several prides may join each other temporarily, forming much larger groups. Usually prides consist of several males and females as well as cubs of various ages. But solitary lions are also common. Females retreat from the group to give birth alone and to nurse the cubs during their first weeks. Then the mothers rejoin the pride, the cubs remaining with them until they are about 18 months old.

I was once able to follow a family of five lions for about forty-eight hours. The family consisted of a male, a female, and three 6-month-old cubs. The preceding night they had killed a topi and eaten most of it. During the entire day after the kill, the adult lions rested, moving only in relation to the sun or to chase vultures from the prey or to go aside to defecate or urinate. The cubs were very active, playing together or with the remains of the dead topi or approaching curiously the grazing kobs and topis in the vicinity. The adult lions did not eat that day but on the second night consumed what remained of the topi carcass. They spent the second day in the same way as the first but no longer troubled to chase the vultures from the carcass. On the third night they went hunting and killed a kob about 300 meters from where they had been resting for forty-eight hours.

When lions are not actively hunting, their herbivorous prey, such as buffaloes and antelopes, have no fear of them; they will graze close to resting lions or as they pass

Above. *Leaping into the air, the bubal hartebeest* (Alcelaphus buselaphus) *seems suspended above the African savanna. The hartebeest is known for its bounding, springing gait and great endurance. Hartebeest is a Boer word for "tough ox." Indeed, the hartebeest is a tough animal.*

Opposite. *Red-billed queleas* (Quelea quelea) *are very gregarious, sometimes flying in flocks of hundreds of thousands. Breeding colonies may contain millions of nests and cover thousands of hectares. These birds inhabit dry grasslands with thorn scrub, but sometimes they enter croplands, where they cause enormous damage, which may even result in famine.*

nearby. In their wanderings, lions may cover up to 30 kilometers in one night. Males of different prides often mingle and hunt within the same area. In parts of Africa with sizable populations of lions there seems to be a kind of rotation of site occupancy, with one pride following another in a given area after a lapse of a day or two. But their habits are very variable in different areas.

Lions try to take their prey by surprise, approaching slowly through the grass until they are close enough to rush the victim. Though the females are swift, they usually give up a chase if they have not overtaken fleeing prey within 50–70 meters. When several lions hunt together their strategy includes occupation of topography so that one lion can drive the prey toward the others. A lion fells smaller prey by striking it with a foreleg or gripping it with its jaws. It leaps onto the back of larger prey, breaking its neck or spinal column with its powerful forepaws or strangling it by biting.

The cheetah (*Acinonyx jubatus*) hunts quite differently. It selects a particular animal in a herd of antelopes and in a crouched position approaches as close to the prey as it can. It then accelerates in a few seconds to a speed of up to 75 kilometers per hour, or even to more than 110 kilometers per hour in the pursuit of a gazelle, impala, or hare. The slender body of the cheetah is catapulted through the air by the long hind legs which stretch forward so far that they strike the ground well in front of the head. If it has not succeeded in overtaking its prey within about a kilometer, it gives up the chase, for it is a short-distance sprinter, whereas gazelles and other antelopes can run longer distances at full speed.

The Hunters: Dogs and Hyenas

In contrast to the cheetahs the wild dogs hunt in packs. Every individual in the group has its special role and these animals display perfect teamwork, especially in the selection of prey—often an ailing animal or a yearling. The wild dog has the reputation of being ferocious and of spreading panic among herbivorous animals wherever it appears. This is undeserved. I have often seen wild dogs resting, playing, or eating while zebras, wildebeest, or other antelopes graze peacefully 15–30 meters away. It is only when they are hunting that they frighten hoofed animals. The latter then know very well what the predators intend.

One morning on the Serengeti Plains when the sun was already high, we met nine wild dogs trotting in single file. We followed them—15–20 meters alongside the pack—in our vehicle for miles over the savanna. The dogs took no notice of us. Gradually we realized that they were headed straight toward a herd of several thousand wildebeest. Only when the dogs were no more than about 60 meters from the herd did the wildebeest begin to move, realizing that the wild dogs had serious business in mind. Both the pack and the herd accelerated until the wildebeest were thundering across the flat savanna in full gallop, the numerous calves easily maintaining the pace. The wild dogs suddenly increased their speed, caught up with the rearguard of the wildebeest, then slowed down a little, running parallel and close to the wildebeest. The wild dogs were testing the antelopes. One of the dogs now made a selection of prey. As it did so, the wildebeest herd

Above. *Swayne's dik-dik* (Madoqua swaynei) *is only slightly larger than a hare. The mostly crepuscular and nocturnal dik-diks inhabit areas where sufficient heavy grass and brush is available for cover.*

Opposite. *Near a water hole, a Thomson's gazelle* (Gazella thomsoni) *encounters a kori bustard* (Ardeotis kori). *This species is the most abundant gazelle in eastern Africa. Like other bustards, the kori bustard prefers to walk or run, but is nevertheless a strong flier.*

86-87 top row, left. *The steenbok (Raphicerus campestris) is one of Africa's smaller antelopes. It is both a grazer and a browser. Steenboks sometimes seek shelter from enemies in aardvark burrows.*

Center. *A female oribi (Ourebia ourebi) stands alert. Oribis inhabit treeless plains, usually near water, throughout much of Africa.*

Right. *Klipspringers (Oreotragus oreotragus) frequent rocky outcroppings, hills, and lava flows scattered about on African plains. Klipspringers, oribis, and steenboks belong to a group called the "pygmy antelopes." They weigh only about 15 kilograms and stand approximately 55 centimeters at the shoulder.*

Center row, left. *Lying in the underbrush, a female gerenuk (Litocranius walleri) displays the long neck with which it reaches the tops of tall bushes and trees to feed on new leaves and shoots. The gerenuk commonly stands on its hind legs, forefeet propped against the tree while it feeds.*

Center. *The kob (Adenota kob) lives in herds that sometimes number 100 animals. These antelopes are not shy; they tend to be highly visible, and do not seek shelter, even in the heat of the day.*

Right. *The gemsbok (Oryx gazella) inhabits dry, desert-like plains of southern Africa, and gets along well without free water, deriving moisture from grasses and ground fruits such as wild melons.*

Bottom. *A male impala (Aepyceros melampus) nuzzles a female. An individual male tries to maintain a harem of several females within his territory. Most harems average less than 20 females, but the number may be several times that. Impalas prefer savanna with light brush and scrub.*

Overleaf. *Streaking through the darkened sky above the Serengeti Plain of Tanzania, lightning illuminates a herd of gazelles.*

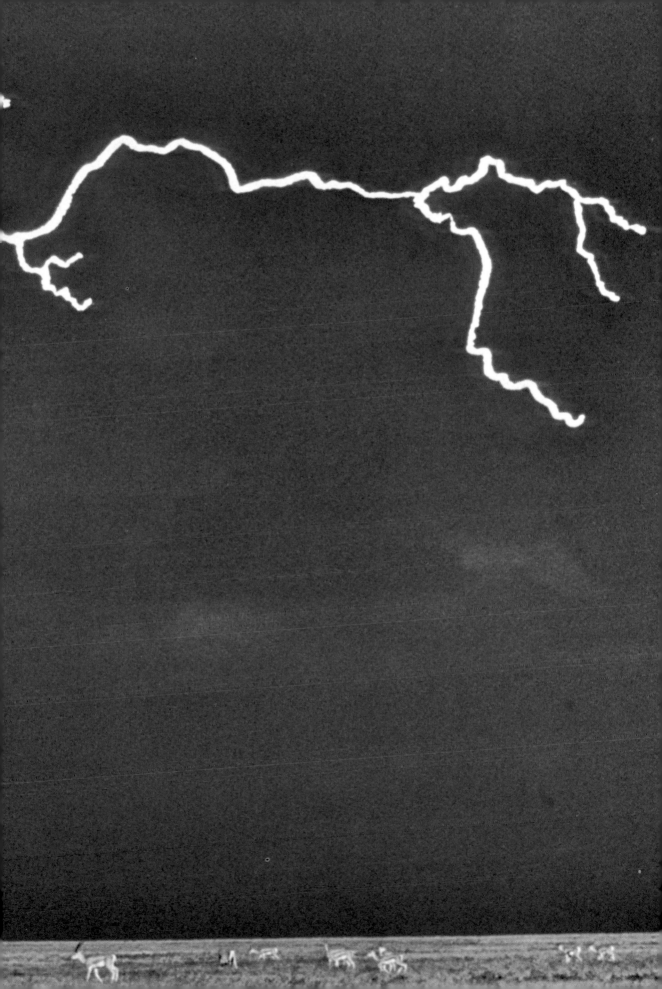

divided in two parts. Without hesitation the wild dogs followed one of the herds, accelerating at an astonishing rate, and broke into the herd. In a moment a quarter-grown calf was cut down.

All the wild dogs began to eat. The wildebeest stopped running but set off again when six of the wild dogs resumed the hunt. In less than a minute a second calf had been selected and killed. Three wild dogs remained at that kill, while three others pursued a lone young Thomson's gazelle (*Gazella thomsoni*) that had become separated from its herd. It was chased for about two minutes—a long run—before it was struck, both the antelope and the predator making a breakneck leap into the air. The wild dogs were now divided into three eating groups. The wildebeest immediately ceased fleeing and began grazing quietly less than 30 meters from the nearest group of wild dogs.

What we had witnessed appeared dramatic, but it was routine for both the wild dogs and the wildebeest.

That was confirmed by the final scene: nine wild dogs resting after their meal were surrounded by grazing wildebeest.

Another animal that is a pack hunter, but was not recognized as such until a few years ago, is the spotted hyena (*Crocuta crocuta*). Observations in the Serengeti and Ngorongoro show that it even preys on big animals such as wildebeest and zebras.

Hyena packs display an organized social hierarchy and are often led by a dominant female. Members of the pack show considerable loyalty to one another and defend their offspring courageously. Of course, the spotted hyena eats carrion, too, but it is not exclusively a scavenger. Often, for that matter, lions scavenge hyena kills.

The other hyenas of Africa are less active hunters. The brown hyena (*Hyaena brunnea*), formerly widely distributed in southern Africa, does take small antelope, but often consumes carrion, even searching sea beaches for dead marine animals. The striped hyena (*H. hyaena*) kills small animals only when it finds nothing to scavenge.

The Unique Aardvark

Among other mammals of the savannas are several strange beasts. One of the great animal "personalities" on the African scene roves drier types of savanna but is rarely seen by human beings because it is active only at night. It is the aardvark (*Orycteropus afer*), an animal so peculiar scientists have given it an order all its own (Tubulidentata). It is a plump creature weighing up to 80 kilograms. It has a long tubular nose with a pig-like snout, long ears, powerful legs, and a muscular tail. It is highly specialized both anatomically and ecologically. Its teeth are small and when those in the front of the jaw are worn down and have been dropped, they are replaced by other teeth further back.

The aardvark is a formidable digger, excavating deep burrows, and its gray-brown skin is often colored entirely red by the lateritic soil in which it works. It is equally efficient in tearing open cement-hard termite nests with the large claws on its forefeet. It needs such tools because it feeds mainly on termites and ants, though it may occasionally consume vegetables. After opening a hole in a termitary, the aardvark inserts its long, sticky, almost

So much of a grassland animal that it avoids even high grass and bush in favor of the shortgrass plains, Thomson's gazelle is extremely abundant. Before departing to feed, a female Thomson's gazelle licks its infant clean to remove any scent. The newborn then hides among the grasses.

Discovered by a cheetah (Acinonyx jubatus), a young Thomson's gazelle runs for its life. Its enemy is a cat that runs faster than any other living land animal. Coursing over the savanna at speeds surpassing 100 kilometers per hour, the cheetah stalks as close as possible to its prey, then bursts into pursuit. The cheetah expends energy quickly, and if a gazelle can twist and turn until the cat is exhausted, it can survive. A young gazelle, however, has little chance. Once the cheetah closes in, it brings down its prey with a forepaw, then kills with a bite to the throat. The chase ended, the cheetah carries off its victim.

snake-like tongue into the mound, and withdraws whatever insects adhere to it. When an aardvark hunts, it makes only one opening in a mound and then proceeds to another mound, covering as much as 15 kilometers in a night. It does not destroy the termitaries.

In Zaïre I have several times come upon aardvark burrows with dozens of entrances and an underground area of about 300 square meters which the aardvarks share with families of warthogs, porcupines, mice, and such birds as nesting little bee-eaters (*Melittophagus pusillus*).

The Lively Baboons

Perhaps the most interesting creatures on the savanna are the baboons. Most widespread is the anubis baboon (*Papio anubis*), with a range almost all across the continent, on a strip of savannas mainly north of the equator.

Baboons live in troops of up to about 100 individuals and are very adaptable; they even have the capacity to live in areas cultivated by man. Baboons feed mainly on the ground, seeking out insects and vegetables. A baboon society has a well-organized hierarchy with a ruling junta of dominant males. These males courageously defend the herd against predators. As baboons cover about 1½–2 kilometers a day, they often meet other animals. Most often the baboons ignore them, but exceptionally they may chase and even kill and eat a gazelle fawn or a young vervet (*Cercopithecus aethiops*). In general, however, baboons do not care for meat. Much of their time is spent in feeding, grooming—an important social function—and sleeping. The nights are spent in trees or on rocks. Babies of all ages are constantly carried around by their mothers, clinging to the parent or casually riding on her back.

An Abundance of Birds

The impressive number of mammals on Africa's savannas has overshadowed the richness of the birdlife. Myriad birds feed on seeds among the grasses, others on insects, and still others hunt their fellow birds, as well as reptiles and rodents and even small or young antelope. No other part of the world has so many different kinds of birds of prey. On the natural African savannas, there are few moments when raptors are not in sight. Often the sky is filled with eagles, hawks, buzzards, and vultures.

Soaring vultures can spot other vultures descending on a carcass at a great distance. In a short time hundreds of vultures of as many as six species may have gathered around the carrion. They will seem to be involved in a hectic scramble, with everyone competing with everyone else. However, each species uses its own technique for reaching a different part of the carcass.

Not all vultures can tear open the tough skin of a dead animal, but once it has been killed by a carnivore, the vultures can eat as soon as they have reached the body, starting on the eyeballs, fleshy muzzle, mouth, and anus. Only after much effort can vultures such as the white-headed vulture (*Trigonoceps occipitalis*) and the lappet-faced vulture (*Torgos tracheliotus*) tear open the skin. Since these two "openers" are the strongest and heaviest of the vultures, they manage to tear off large segments of the carcass. After this has been done the other vultures move in. The white-backed vultures (*Gyps africanus*) are

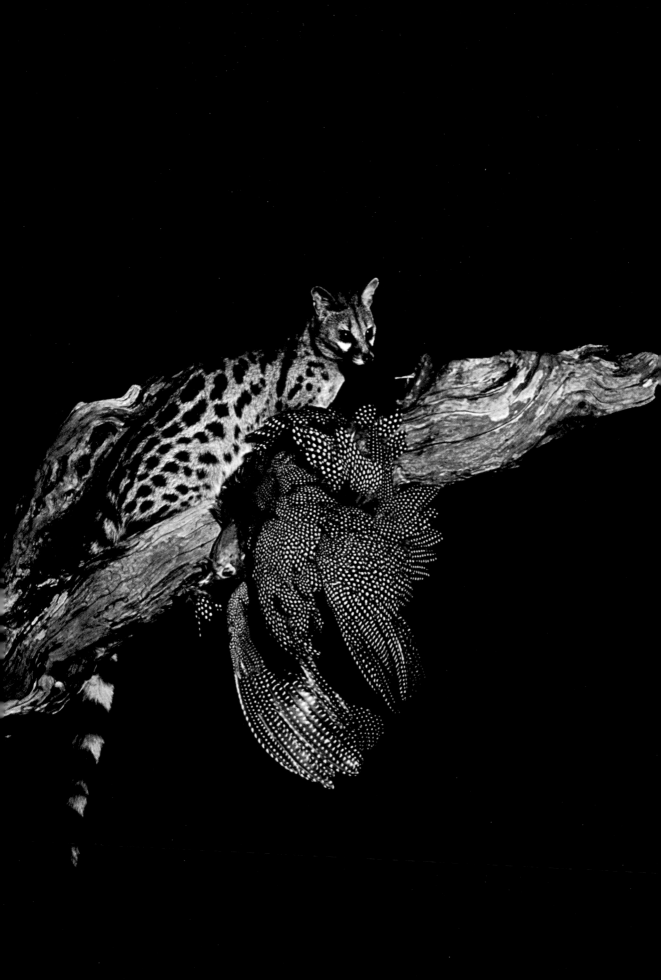

almost always in the majority around a kill. Equipped with long, featherless necks, they are able to rip out fleshy parts from deep inside the carcass. Rüppell's vulture (*G. rüppelli*) also works in this way, but it is not so common. Finally, the two smallest vultures, the hooded vulture (*Necrosyrtes monachus*) and the Egyptian vulture (*Neophron percnopterus*), pick up smaller pieces or clean the meat from the bones. If lions are eating, all the vultures must wait until they have finished, but vultures often eat simultaneously with hyenas, jackals, and marabou storks.

A grotesque-looking bird, the marabou stork (*Leptoptilus crumeniferus*) is a scavenger, as well as a hunter of whatever small creatures it can snap up in its huge beak. It commonly roosts in trees at night, soaring or standing on the ground by day.

Ground-dwelling birds are common in the savannas, along with arboreal species in the scattered trees or bushes. Most visible among the ground dwellers are tall birds like the secretary bird (*Sagittarius secretarius*), guinea fowl of various species, bustards, and the ostrich (*Struthio camelus*). The secretary bird is over a meter tall and stalks about on long, stilt-like legs. It got its name because of its crest feathers, which resemble quill pens that were stuck behind the ears of secretaries and clerks of earlier days. Secretary birds walk for miles through the grass in search of food. Sometimes they stamp on the ground to frighten mice into moving. But the secretary bird has also become famous as an efficient snake killer. It will attack snakes as long as 2 meters, delivering powerful blows with the feet while holding its wings outspread as a shield against the snake's counterattack. Sometimes there is a struggle, but the secretary bird dominates.

The ostrich, the largest living bird—over 2 meters tall and weighing up to 150 kilograms—inhabits the open savannas of Africa. It cannot fly, but its long, powerful legs can deliver deadly blows and enable it to run as fast as 70 kilometers an hour. Its extraordinarily sharp vision also helps it detect enemies at a great distance. Ostriches are usually found in small groups, in pairs, or singly. They frequently associate with herds of antelopes and zebras. In such gatherings the ostrich often serves as a sentinel because it can detect danger sooner than any of the herbivores except the giraffe. Like these mammals, ostriches feed on plants, especially succulents, as well as seeds and berries. They are polygamous, the male mating with three or four females. He selects the nest site and scratches a shallow pit in which all his females lay their eggs. Such collective clutches consist of 12–20 eggs but instances of about 100 eggs in one nest, each weighing about 1.5 kilograms, have been reported. Only one female takes care of the brooding, while the other females desert the area. The male remains with the "head female," defending the nest and incubating by night. This division is practical since by day the brownish female is more difficult to detect than the blackish male. When approached by a man or a hyena she tries to make herself as inconspicuous as possible, stretching her neck along the ground. When herds of elephants, antelopes, or zebras approach, the female flaps her wings, moves around, and does her utmost to announce her presence. She thus

Overleaf. A male and female lion (Panthera leo) greet each other. By far the most social of all cats, lions usually live in groups called prides, which sometimes number several dozen individuals. The pride is ruled by a dominant male, who is often aided by a few other males allied with him—a royal bodyguard of sorts. Each pride maintains its own territory, which is defended—sometimes in bloody combat—against other groups of lions.

Above. A vulturine guinea fowl (Acryllium vulturinum) peers into the bush of northern Kenya. Living on dry grasslands, it undergoes sharp fluctuations in population, sometimes being rare, at other times extremely abundant.

Opposite. A sleek large-spotted genet (Genetta tigrina) has killed a crested guineafowl (Guttera edouardi) and taken it into a tree. The genet has several cat-like characteristics, including retractile claws, but belongs to a family known as the viverrids, which also includes the mongooses and civets. This species ranges through most of subsaharan Africa, in both forest and bushy grassland.

manages to have the herbivores make a detour around the nest. But ostrich eggs are preyed upon by some mammals and birds. Hyenas, for instance, crush the shells easily. In a remarkable example of an animal using a tool, Egyptian vultures use a stone to break ostrich eggs. The bird may bring the stone from a distance of 20–30 meters or so and drop it on the egg until it cracks.

Other striking ground birds on the southern woodland savannas include the ground hornbill (*Bucorvus leadbeateri*), Denham's bustard (*Neotis denhami*), wattled crane (*Bugeranus carunculatus*), southern carmine bee-eater (*Merops nubicoides*), white-fronted bee-eater (*Melittophagus bullockoides*), and helmeted guinea fowl (*Numida meleagris mitrata*). Wintering yellow wagtails (*Motacilla flava*) occur over practically all shortgrass areas of tropical Africa from park lawns and airports to grassland and woodland savannas. Like cattle egrets (*Ardeola ibis*), these birds are especially attracted to herds of cattle and wild hoofed mammals. Advancing slowly in the grass, the grazing mammals stir up insects, which yellow wagtails are quick to consume. The wagtails are migrants from virtually all of Eurasia, where they breed as far north as the tundra's edge.

Small birds called oxpeckers often accompany the larger herbivores, climbing around on their flanks searching for ticks and other parasites. Of the two species of oxpeckers, the yellow-billed (*Buphagus africanus*) has the widest range in northern, eastern, and southern savannas, while the red-billed oxpecker (*B. erythrorhynchus*) is restricted to eastern Africa from the Sudan to South Africa. Even when ungulates gallop at full speed the birds hang on.

The Ubiquitous Insects

There are myriad insects on the savannas: beetles, bees, and wasps abound but even more characteristic of the region are locusts, grasshoppers, ants, and termites. In various shapes and forms, termite mounds dot the savannas, even though many termite species build nests below the ground or in trees. Most species build a subterranean structure or simply live either in the soil or in the woody parts of plants. Many species of termites are grass eaters, dragging dry grass underground and consuming it there. This and other termite activities aerate the soil and let water filter through it. In certain savanna areas termite mounds are very large, sometimes as much as 8 meters high and 10 meters around the rust-colored base. They are as hard as cement, astonishingly durable, withstanding decades or even centuries of rain, wind, and sand erosion. During wars in Africa, termitaries have frequently been used as miniature fortresses and gun turrets. Large termite hills are sophisticated air-conditioned structures in which fungi help keep an almost constant temperature and regulate humidity through bacterial fermentation. These fungus gardens may also absorb moisture and release it when humidity decreases.

Locusts often sweep the African savannas. When the adults have depleted their food resources they set out on migration, riding the winds for 17 hours at a stretch. In a single season, swarms can travel up to 3000 kilometers. Heavy rains in normally arid regions may give rise to outbursts of locust populations.

Above. *Lionesses are watchful mothers. There are usually from two to four cubs in a litter, and the cubs remain with their mother for about a year and a half.*

Opposite. *A lion pair mates. The dominant male and his cronies have the right to mate with any receptive females in the pride. Females are in heat for about a week each month, except during pregnancy.*

101

103 top. *African hunting dogs* (Lycaon pictus) *devour a Grant's gazelle* (Gazella granti) *on the Serengeti Plain. Hunting dogs live in packs that usually number about a dozen individuals, although packs may contain as many as 40 members. As among wolves, the wild dogs' hunting tactics are highly organized. They use relays to run down prey and employ decoying behavior to trick their victims.*

Center. *The yapping of black-backed jackals* (Canis mesomelas) *can be heard on Africa's open plains and bush country. Jackals are scavengers, but also kill small animals such as game birds and sometimes even antelopes.*

Bottom. *A spotted hyena* (Crocuta crocuta) *lopes across the savanna. The hyena was long thought to be purely a scavenger, but recent research shows it is also a superb hunter, often working in packs and bringing down prey as large as zebras and wildebeests.*

Overleaf. *Vultures* (Gyps) *constantly patrol the African plains, searching with keen eyes for carrion. Once an abandoned kill is sighted, vultures alight in droves to feast upon the remains.*

Deadly Mambas and Other Reptiles

With a rich insect and rodent life and plenty of underground shelters in various animal-made cavities, savannas also provide habitats for reptiles. The reptiles are mostly snakes and lizards, but there are also a few species of turtles. Among the savanna snakes, the cobras, vipers, and mambas are the best known, because of their deadly bites.

Mambas are supposed to be exceedingly aggressive, but like most snakes, they normally do not attack humans unless cornered or provoked. Many attempts by snakes to escape into a hole which may be next to the intruder have been misinterpreted as deliberate aggression. The mambas are famous in Africa also for being extremely poisonous and extraordinarily swift. Since one of the two species, the black mamba (*Dendroaspis polylepis*), may grow to 4.27 meters, it is an impressive snake, and is the most feared of all African reptiles. There are hair-raising stories about the ferocity of mambas and their deadliness, but these are usually grossly overdramatized. It is true, however, that the venom of mambas may cause unconsciousness and death in a few minutes.

Its relative, the green mamba (*D. angusticeps*), attains a length of only about 2 meters. Both species move with incredible speed when trying to escape intruders. In trees the slender mambas give the impression of almost flying between the branches. On the ground they appear as rope-like objects moving away at great speed or throwing up little clouds of dust. This snake has been timed at 11 kilometers an hour over a distance of 43 meters. Green mambas are seldom seen, because they are mainly arboreal, but they do have shelters and hunt rodents on the ground. The black mamba is more at home in open bush country and is therefore easier to observe.

Some savannas are inhabited by Africa's two most venomous snakes, the boomslang (*Dispholidus typus*) and the twig snake (*Thelothornis kirtlandii*). The venom of these reptiles affects both the nervous and blood systems. However, since both are back-fanged species, it is almost impossible for them to inflict fatal bites unless they are handled in such a way that they can bite with the corner of the mouth.

Of the nonvenomous snakes, the African rock python (*Python sebae*) is known for reaching a length of up to 7 meters. One evening at sunset I was in a thicket at the edge of a savanna in eastern Zaïre watching a small track made by such animals as ratels (*Mellivora capensis*), civets, (*Viverra civetta*), and porcupines. Suddenly I detected about 15 meters away a small animal coming toward me. Just as I saw it, the animal was struck by a snake. The blow was so strong that the mammal was knocked sideways more than a meter. Immediately the snake—an African rock python—was on its prey, literally covering it with its powerful coils.

Slowly I approached the animals. The fight was already over. The prey was so well covered by the coils of the python, which was almost 2 meters long, that I was unable to determine whether it was an adult banded mongoose (*Mungos mungo*) or a young greater mongoose (*Herpestes ichneumon*). The python saw me but showed no sign of releasing its prey and it soon became too dark to make further observations. The whole action happened

Above. *The polygamous male ostrich* (Struthio camelus) *sometimes mates with as many as four females. Eggs are laid in a shallow communal nest.*

Left. *An ostrich egg, which may weigh 1.5 kilograms, hatches after six weeks. The young are able to run almost as soon as they emerge.*

A young chacma baboon (Papio ursinus) *picks up an ostrich egg and lugs it away from the nest (above). It then sucks out the egg's contents (right).*

108

in a flash. Presumably the python was waiting beside the path and reacted to "microvibrations" of the ground when the mongoose trotted past.

I could not tell whether the python struck with open or closed jaws. In general, pythons are said to strike mainly in self-defense. Perhaps the python's methods of capturing prey are more varied than has been assumed.

The most common savanna snakes are species of sand snakes; the most abundant, *Psammophis sibilans*, often sunbathes on grass tussocks or bushes. Sand snakes are even swifter than mambas. In contrast to the slender, diurnal sand snakes, the earth snakes of two genera, *Typhlops* and *Leptotyphlops*, are practically blind and look like giant earthworms. They live underground and feed mainly on termites and ants.

Lizards have developed a much higher heat resistance than snakes and are therefore particularly well represented in the open savannas; but they prefer areas with trees, bushes, rocks, or termite hills from which they can monitor their territories. Skinks (*Mabuya*), agamas (*Agama*), and monitor lizards (*Varanus*) are most conspicuous. There are many known species of agama lizards in Africa and nearly all of them are known for their ability to change color as part of their territorial behavior, nuptial ceremonies, or any form of excitement. Several species, such as the diurnal tree agama (*Agama atricollis*), breed throughout the year, which means that males must constantly defend their territory. They guard their territory from the top of elevated sites, which are usually exposed to direct sunlight for about twelve hours each day. They endure the high temperatures as long as they can, but finally seek shaded places. The maximum temperature tolerance of *A. atricollis* lies within the range of 43–43.9 degrees C. but the preferred upper limit is somewhat lower—42.5 degrees C. As soon as their body temperatures have cooled off in the shade, they return to their lookout in the sun.

Courtship of females and aggressive displays to ward off intruding males are also performed on these sites. The males bob their vivid blue heads up and down, making these territorial guardians very conspicuous. The bobbing is performed so frequently that it is surprising that male tree agamas do not fall victim to avian raptors more often. Despite many days of watching agamas in Zaïre, I have never seen them attacked by the numerous birds of prey in the same habitats. However, elsewhere I have seen other species of agamas preyed upon by dark chanting-goshawks (*Melierax metabates*).

A Reminder of the Past

From highly evolved mammals such as antelopes and elephants, to cold-blooded ones such as lizards and serpents, the life of the African grasslands is rich and exceedingly varied, even today. Increasingly, however, mushrooming human populations and their demands for food and living space, together with the pressures from industry for mineral resources such as ores, are eating away at the immense African savannas. Where savannas can be kept in something like their natural state, however, they are constant reminders of what the world was like long, long ago and also of the immensity of their productivity.

Overleaf. *Riding its mother's back, a young Anubis baboon* (Papio anubis) *surveys the savanna. The anubis inhabits savannas across the middle of Africa, mostly north of the equator. Typical of baboons, it lives in troops with a well-established pecking order. Males lead and guard the troop while the females attend to the young.*

Australia: Grasslands of a Continent Apart

Grasslands dominate the landscape of Australia. Almost half the land surface of the continent—47 percent—is grassland, although some areas are so dry they look as sere as the desert at the continent's heart. Lack of moisture is a crucial fact of life in Australia. One third of the continent has an average rainfall of only 352 millimeters annually. Droughts that grip the grasslands tend to be prolonged; the periods of rain brief.

Since a sizable part of Australia lies north of the Tropic of Capricorn, and the mass of the continent spans almost 15 degrees of latitude in the South Temperate Zone, a fair amount of variation occurs in the grasslands despite their general aridity. The pattern ranges from tropical savanna in the north to dry plains in the interior. The dry plains, together with scrublands, virtually surround the central desert of Australia. There are two main types of scrub, one dominated by the acacia known as mulga (*Acacia aneura*), another made up mainly of dwarf eucalypts, known as mallee scrub. Such scrublands are dry but can have, especially in the south, a rich growth of grass. Southern species include wallaby grass (*Danthonia caespitosa*) and feather grass (*Stipa*), while in the northern regions Mitchell grass (*Astrebla elymoides*) replaces the wallaby grass. When it rains, flowers appearing in the grasses of the scrublands blaze into a patchwork of yellow, white, pink, and violet.

Another type of scrub found in the interior of Australia is dominated by saltbushes, such as *Atriplex*, together with bluebushes (*Rhagodia*), berry saltbushes (*Nitraria*), and occasionally desert oak (*Casuarina decaisneana*). This area, adjacent to the central desert, is almost as dry as the Sahara, but bursts into greenery when the rare rains come. The broadest expanse of grasslands on the continent lies between the Great Dividing Range in the east and the central desert in the west. The largest portion of these is covered by spinifex grassland, consisting mainly of porcupine grass (*Triodia*), which is prickly and tough, and adapted to this area, which, although not as dry as the saltbush landscape, is more arid than mulga and mallee scrub.

The original character of many Australian grasslands has been lost due to conversion into pasture or farmland. Much of the native vegetation has been replaced by introduced plants, which together with introduced animals have completely changed the ecology in many places.

Animals from Abroad

At least 17 wild mammals have been introduced in Australia since the continent was settled by Europeans in 1788. The wild rabbit (*Oryctolagus cuniculus*), brought to Australia in 1859, was perhaps the most destructive of the newcomers. These rabbits multiplied explosively and exterminated many species of grassland plants.

Added to the havoc wrought by wild alien animals has been that caused by domestic stock, especially sheep. Sheep ranching in certain parts of western New South Wales has changed to shortgrass a shrubby saltbush vegetation mixed with myall (*Acacia homalophylla*) and other trees.

Because it has been isolated from other continents for many ages, Australia has been a refuge for highly specialized plants as well as animals, such as marsupials.

113

Above. *Certain grasses, such as kangaroo grass* (Themeda australis), *have evolved a reproductive adaptation in the arrangement of their flower spikes. The flowers are ordered so that the seeds detach and scatter over the ground.*

Opposite. *The pretty-face wallaby* (Wallabia parryi) *is a grass-eating herd animal that prefers open areas with light tree cover. It is named for its elegant facial markings.*

As a rule, such isolated, highly specialized species are very vulnerable to competition from introduced types and the ecological imbalance that results from their appearance. Many marsupials, for example, have vanished since Europeans arrived with their plants and animals. The original mammals of the saltbush plains are unknown because the habitats were completely altered by livestock before anyone took note of the wild fauna. The hairy-nosed wombat (*Lasiorhinus altifrons*) may be the only original saltbush survivor among the larger mammals. Originally, however, a multitude of marsupials thrived on Australian grasslands, filling niches taken on grasslands elsewhere in the world by the more advanced placental mammals. Kangaroos, for instance, play much the same role on Australian grasslands as hoofed animals do in Africa.

Mobs of Kangaroos
Kangaroos are the largest members of the family Macropodidae, which also includes wallabies and rat kangaroos (*Bettongia*). Among the best known are the euro or wallaroo (*Macropus robustus*), the red kangaroo (*M. rufus*), and the eastern gray kangaroo (*M. giganteus*) and western gray kangaroo (*M. fuliginosus*). The gray kangaroo male may reach a length of 2.5 meters, including the tail. Kangaroos can stand erect, with the tail acting like the third leg of a tripod. But all of a kangaroo's dignity seems to disappear when it begins to move with its peculiar hopping gait. At first sight the movement seems awkward, but it soon becomes apparent that this bouncing motion is both practical and quite beautiful. Kangaroos can bound at speeds as great as 55 kilometers per hour, clear fences 3 meters high, and make horizontal leaps of 9 meters. When kangaroos are feeding, they bound about as though in slow motion.
The red kangaroo lives in mobs of 12–15 or more. Sometimes the males fight, looking almost exactly like two human beings boxing. Standing erect, they ward off each other with their forelegs. They also kick with both hind legs simultaneously while resting on the muscular tail.
One of the most remarkable features in the biology of kangaroos is their reproduction. Usually they give birth to only one young, but can keep an embryo in reserve in case the newborn does not survive. After a short gestation period without placental connection between mother and embryo, the latter is born in a very embryonic stage, hairless, blind, and deaf. Even in the largest kangaroos the offspring at birth is no bigger than a mouse, while in smaller wallabies it is bean-sized. At birth the embryo has almost no hind legs but the forefeet are equipped with claws. After birth, this tiny creature, without assistance, uses its forefeet to climb from the genital opening upward to the maternal pouch. In some species the mother prepares the way by licking a "path" through her thick hair. The embryo's travel may take from three minutes to a full hour, during which the mother remains as quiet as possible. After the embryo has reached the entrance to the pouch, it climbs inside and attaches its mouth to one of the teats. It remains in this position for several weeks while embryonic development continues. The young then uses the pouch as a temporary refuge for 8–11 months,

long after it has begun to graze and has grown almost as large as its mother.

On the Australian grasslands, kangaroos have been mistakenly accused of competing with sheep. Since 1964 about one to two million kangaroos have been slaughtered each year, particularly in areas where the red kangaroo and the euro are considered competitors with sheep for grazing. In Western Australia poisoning campaigns have been conducted against the euro because it was said to hinder pasture-regeneration programs. But scientists found that the primary cause of the deterioration of the pastures was not marsupials but overgrazing by sheep. Kangaroos grow fat on the apparently poor fodder of dry grasslands, and, if they have shade, they can do without water. Although they reproduce quickly, their occasional high mortality causes their numbers to drop considerably, giving pasture an opportunity to recover. In other words, the kangaroos are in balance with their habitat; the sheep were not. The farmers themselves were responsible for the loss of good pasture by burning the grass during the sheep roundup season when nutritious plants carried seed. The farmers also tended to overstock and to concentrate sheep in the same areas year after year, so the flocks overgrazed the land.

The Dingo

Another animal that has been treated as a pest because of the problems it poses to sheep is the dingo (*Canis dingo*), the so-called Australian wild dog. It is not a native of Australia but came there from Asia. There is evidence that the dingo was in Australia about 11,000 years ago; it then disappeared but returned 5000 years later. Whether the dingo was introduced once or several times, it probably had a devastating effect on many native animals, because, unlike other continents with large fauna, Australia has few other predatory mammals. Until recently, the only large predator in Australia was the thylacine wolf (*Thylacinus cynocephalus*), whose rapid extinction may have resulted from competition with the dingo. When Europeans arrived in Tasmania, thylacines were still there, but were found only in forests. They may never have been true grassland dwellers, so that when the dingo appeared on the savannas and steppes of Australia, the herbivores probably met a predator for the first time.

Parrots, Mallee Fowl, and Other Birds

Many birds have adapted to the dry climate of Australian grasslands. A huge number of these birds are nomadic rather than migratory or resident, wandering wherever erratic rains yield optimal conditions. The scrub, grassland, and light-wooded savannas are inhabited by a wide variety of such birds, many living in flocks, at least during certain seasons. Parrots are very well represented in Australia and many more species have adapted to grassy plains than have the parrots of other continents. Red-rumped parrots (*Psephotus haematonotus*) in green and red, blue-bonnet parrots (*P. haematogaster*), and especially green budgerigars (*Melopsittacus undulatus*) fly around in large flocks, their colorful plumage enlivening the vast grassland expanses.

Rose-breasted cockatoos (*Cacatua roseicapilla*), pink sulphur-crested cockatoos (*C. galerita*), and gray and

white cockateels (*Leptolophus hollandicum*) fly noisily between feeding sites on the ground, where they eat succulent plants, seeds, and roots. Yellow rosellas (*Platycercus flaveolus*) add yet more color to the plain. Unfortunately, the attractive paradise parrot (*Psephotus pulcherrimus*), which nests in termite mounds, and the scarlet-crested parrot (*Neophema splendida*) have decreased considerably.

Bustards are true birds of the grasslands, but only one species occurs in Australia, in contrast to the 18 species in Africa. Like all its relatives, the Australian bustard (*Eupodotis australis*) lives almost entirely on the ground. Even when disturbed it runs away rather than taking wing. It is a great consumer of grasshoppers, but it has nevertheless been recklessly persecuted by hunters and introduced foxes and dogs. It survives only in remote areas. Here again we see that alterations of the grasslands caused by rabbits and sheep have probably contributed to the decline of this valuable bird.

The history of the flock pigeon (*Histriophaps histrionica*) resembles that of the North American passenger pigeon (*Ectopistes migratorius*). Millions of these nomadic birds once congregated on the grassy plains of northern Australia, New South Wales, and northern South Australia. Immense flocks visited drinking pools, where they became easy prey for hunters. Fortunately the population has recently shown signs of recovery in some places.

Surprisingly, the wedge-tailed eagle (*Aquila audax*), the largest of Australia's birds of prey and an inhabitant of the plains, seems to have withstood constant persecution (although it once dwindled almost to extinction). Over 30,000 of these birds are killed each year throughout Australia under the pretext that they are harmful to lambs. A high percentage of the sheep eaten by these eagles is surely carrion. Every year in Australia, 10 million newborn lambs die of starvation because the suckling relationship between mother and offspring has been broken or was never established. This abundance of carrion probably explains why wedge-tailed eagles survive so well. The natural prey of the wedge-tailed eagle used to be wallabies, but today rabbits constitute its primary diet, so that reducing the eagle population appears to be an illogical policy.

Among the birds that prefer dry grasslands are the stone curlew (*Burhinus grallarius*) and the black-breasted plover (*Zonifer tricolor*) as well as pigeons, button quails (*Turnix*), quails, larks, field wrens, and others. Woodland savanna species include the rufous song lark (*Cicloramphus mathewsi*)—commoner here than in the open grassland—the lovely wren (*Malurus amabilis*), several species of honey eaters and the pale-headed rosella (*Platycercus adscitus*). Typical mallee scrub birds include quail thrushes (*Cinclosoma*), robins, wrens and whistlers, about twenty species of honey eaters, the tree martin (*Hylochelidon nigricans*)—a species that is found almost everywhere in Australia—the princess parakeet (*Polytelis alexandrae*)—beautifully colored in green, yellow, and red—and the pink cockatoo (*Cacatua leadbeateri*).

The emu (*Dromaius novaehollandiae*) was once found in almost all habitats. But emus prefer grasslands, where

Above. *The red-rumped parrot* (Psephotus haematonotus) *is a common species that often nests in the abandoned nests of Australian bee-eaters* (Merops ornatus).

Opposite. *Parrots, parakeets, and their relatives thrive in Australia. Some of them, especially parakeets and budgerigars, are extremely common. Others, such as the turquoise grass parakeet* (Neophema pulchella), *have undergone a rapid decline due to the pet trade.*

they stalk around in small groups. Australia's largest bird, the emu can weigh up to 55 kilograms and stand 180 centimeters tall. When pursued they flee at speeds of up to 55 kilometers per hour. The male emu is charged with rearing the young, which hatch from eggs placed by several different females in a nest—hardly more than a leaf-lined depression in the ground—built by the male. Until the young can move on their own, he herds and stands guard over them.

Here and there, the "incubating" mounds that the mallee hen, or mallee fowl (*Leipoa ocellata*), builds of sand and plant debris may be seen. This bird relies on decaying vegetation and the sun to warm and hatch its eggs, and it has attracted much attention by the remarkable way it regulates the heat of the mound by manipulating the leaves and other materials in it. The male has an extremely taxing job. Although the outside temperatures may vary as much as 40 degrees C., the temperature inside the mound must remain around 33.5 degrees C. If it is too hot, the bird must open the mound to let it cool off. When temperatures dip, he must pile on more debris. Work on the mound goes on for most of the year—all but a month or so, in fact. It takes the male four months to prepare it; then the eggs are laid. It takes at least another seven months before they hatch, and all this time he must stand by, visiting the nest regularly to keep tabs on the temperature, which he probably senses through his beak.

Some birds are specialized to the mulga association of acacias. Such are the gray honey eater (*Conopophila whitei*), robust thornbill (*Acanthiza robustirostris*), white-browed tree creeper (*Climacteris affinis*), and perhaps the mulga parrot (*Psephotus varius*). Two characteristic bird species of the saltbush are the orange chat (*Epthianura aurifrons*) and white-winged wren (*Malurus leucopterus*).

Monitor Lizards and Death Adders

Australia has a rich fauna of lizards and snakes. The most spectacular of its lizards are the monitors (Varanidae), a family that is widespread in the Old World. But half of all species of monitors inhabit Australia.

There is great variation in size among Australian monitors. The smallest, *Varanus brevicauda*, measures only 20 centimeters. The largest, the perentie (*V. giganteus*), can be 244 centimeters long. There are also many differences in terms of habits. One species of monitors, *V. gilleni*, lives in trees; others are terrestrial or semi-aquatic. Some, such as the water monitor (*V. salvator*), are versatile and are at home in trees, on the ground, in water, or underground.

Monitor feeding habits are also diverse. Some consume insects; others eggs and young birds. The largest monitors are capable of killing medium-sized mammals. They use teeth and claws to tear their prey into chunks, and then swallow the pieces whole. Monitors also eat considerable amounts of carrion, which they find by scent. In a way, the monitors fill the scavenging role of jackals and hyenas on the Australian grasslands. Almost all monitors also have a formidable weapon in their tail, which they wield like a whip and with tremendous force.

To Australians all monitors are "goannas," a misnomer

Above, opposite. *Emus* (Dromaius novaehollandiae) *feed on both insects and vegetation, and range grasslands and lightly wooded areas, seldom far from water. They can, however, subsist without water for quite some time, and are found even on the hot desert of central Australia. Males build the nests, incubate the eggs, and rear the young.*

Overleaf. *The Australian bustard* (Choriotis australis) *is now protected by law, but once was heavily hunted. The bustard nests on the ground; after the eggs hatch, the chicks go off with the female. When an enemy approaches, the female slinks away, leaving the chicks alone. They flatten to the ground and freeze, making it virtually impossible for a predator to see them.*

deriving from the word "iguana," another family of lizards that does not even appear in Australia. The only similarity between the two families is the large size of some members, although no iguana reaches the bulk of the largest monitor.

Male monitor lizards indulge in impressive ritual combats. Rearing up on their hind legs, they grapple with their front legs until one is pushed over. The teeth are never used in these battles.

The dry spinifex grasslands are full of agama lizards, skinks, and numerous small snakes. Australia has more agamids than any other part of the world. They are well adapted to the hot Australian environment. Australia is in fact host to the largest number of heat-tolerant reptiles in the world, with 16 species tolerating body temperatures above 43 degrees C. The most famous agamid lizard of Australia, the thorny devil (*Moloch horridus*), resembles the American horned toad (*Phrynosoma*), another bizarre-looking lizard, whose body is covered with spines and spiny tubercles.

Of the several impressive serpents found in Australia, a number range the grasslands, although none is exclusively associated with this biome. Some of them are among the most venomous in the world: the death adder (*Acanthopis antarcticus*), brown snake (*Demansia textilis*), and mulga snake (*Pseudechis australis*). Inhabiting mostly the grasslands and savannas of northern Australia—although it also occurs in New Guinea—is a creature that is a candidate for the title of the world's most dangerous snake. The taipan (*Oxyuranus scutellatus*) reaches an average length of 2 meters, although some specimens grow to almost twice that length. It has huge fangs, and is so fast it can strike several times before a victim has a chance to move. Its venom is one of the most toxic known, and until an antivenom was developed a few years ago, few people survived the taipan's bite.

The home of dangerous serpents, lizards in abundance, and some of the world's most primitive mammals, the grasslands of Australia have been a land apart from the rest of the world. Like wild places everywhere, however, they have felt the presence and pressures of man.

Where the Bison Roamed: North America

North American grasslands are dominated by the vast prairie belt. This zone stretches 3700 kilometers on a north-south axis, from Alberta, Saskatchewan, and Manitoba in Canada to the Gulf of Mexico in Texas. Beginning just east of the Mississippi River, with outliers even in Ohio and Indiana, the prairies reach west to the Rocky Mountains, or at least they once did in their natural state. West of the Rockies, in places such as the Great Basin of Utah and Nevada, and in Arizona, New Mexico, and northern Mexico, lie the more arid grasslands. Here grasses grow along with sagebrush (*Artemisia tridentata*) and mesquite (*Prosopis juliflora*) communities. Such country verges on desert, and is much less fertile than the prairie belt, which has marvelously rich soil.

The Prairie and the Bison

The rich soil of the prairie is the main reason that so little of the original prairie remains. Farming and ranching have taken over most of it, and much of it has become industrialized or urbanized. It is almost impossible to find prairie areas untouched by man. No reserve in Canada or the United States was set aside before the westward tide of settlement swept this grassland.

Little more than a century ago, the prairies were largely wilderness, the home of perhaps 60 million American bison, maybe the most numerous large mammal known in historical times. That the prairie could support such herds, along with millions of other animals, demonstrates the abundance of food it provided—that is, when its ecology was in balance, as it was before humans disturbed it.

Although the range of the bison stretched beyond the boundaries of the prairie zone, this species set the tone for the ecological harmony on the prairie. When whites began to settle North America, some bison ranged as far east as the Appalachian Mountains, but the center of their domain was from the Mississippi to the Rockies.

Bison used the prairie in cyclic fashion, on both a daily and a longer-term basis. The animals regularly grazed in the morning, then moved to a water hole to rest and ruminate during midday. In the evening, they resumed grazing. Usually a herd—which might range up to as many as a few million animals—would feed in one area for a week or two, then move on to another when the pasture began to thin out. Thus no one place was overgrazed.

Weighing more than a ton, with some of them standing almost 2 meters high at the shoulder, the bison needs considerable amounts of forage. It was able to sustain itself without overgrazing because it is adapted to eating an exceedingly wide variety of vegetation. Domestic cattle, by way of comparison, can digest only a few types of natural prairie vegetation, and so use the grassland inefficiently.

One of the adaptations of bison to prairie life is the ability to withstand winter cold, snow, and even the howling blizzards that sometimes sweep the plains. When the storms challenge, the bison lowers its shaggy head, facing directly into the teeth of the wind. The huge animal has much more hair on the front of its body, thus the wisdom of turning that end into the storm, rather than fleeing before it like the Eurasian saiga antelope, which must cope with weather of similar severity.

Above. *Clustered on the wintry South Dakota prairie, a herd of bison* (Bison bison) *forages. Using its huge head as a plow, the bison sweeps aside snow to obtain grass and other vegetation.*

Opposite. *When blizzards howl, the bison faces directly into the wind. The species can tolerate winter weather as cold as that of interior Alaska and northern Canada.*

The huge head of the bison helps it find food in winter, when the forage is often deep beneath the snow. It shoves its snout into the snow, and sweeps its head from one side to another, heaving the snow away and gaining access to the grass.

If a thaw melts part of the snow, and is then followed by a freeze, the bison's method of plowing snow cover away fails to work. Such conditions harden the surface of the snow into an icy crust, which often the bison cannot sweep aside with its head. This is one of the only winter conditions that threaten healthy adult bison. Even temperatures of minus 40 degrees C. do not seem to harm them.

Nor, for that matter, do summer temperatures that edge above 38 degrees C. seem to bother the bison. It can withstand the baking sun of the Great Plains as well as the icy cold.

Summer is the breeding season for the bison. As it approaches, the bulls become aggressive toward one another. The usual aim of a bull is to try to take charge of a herd of females, although other males will continually attempt to steal them. A battle between two bulls is awesome. Shaking their shaggy heads, they fence from a distance at first, pawing the ground and stirring up a whirlwind of dust. Then they meet, head to head, shoving, heaving, and hooking with their shining, fearfully sharp horns. After successive charges and batterings, the stronger bull usually wins. If his challenger approaches him in power, however, they may fight several battles before dominance is decided.

Bison are born in the spring, after a gestation that takes approximately as long as that of a human embryo. The weight of a calf at birth may be as much as 32 kilograms, but usually it is somewhat less. The youngster can stand at birth but needs a few days before it can walk firmly. The mother and the rest of the herd guard it from harm.

The great bison herds offered an endless supply of living resources for the American Indians of the prairies, but were little utilized until the arrival of Europeans. Ironically, the ability of the Indians to hunt the bison reached its zenith only after the coming of Europeans to North America and the introduction of the domestic horse. With horses, the Indians could pursue the bison effectively and so an entirely new economy based on bison hunting arose among the prairie tribes. Not only did the bison provide food, but its hide was made into extraordinarily warm clothing.

Hunting by Indians took only minimal numbers of bison, in no way affecting the survival of the species. It was only after the whites reached the prairies that the bison herds began to dwindle. The animals were slaughtered first for meat and hides, then as a political weapon to force the Indians to depend on government beef, which they obtained when they settled on reservations.

By the last decades of the nineteenth century the bison was on the verge of extinction. At the last moment, a drive was begun by conservationists to save the animal. Preserves were established, populated largely by animals that had been sheltered in captivity, mostly at the Bronx Zoo in New York City. Today, the descendants of such animals, living in national parks, preserves, and private

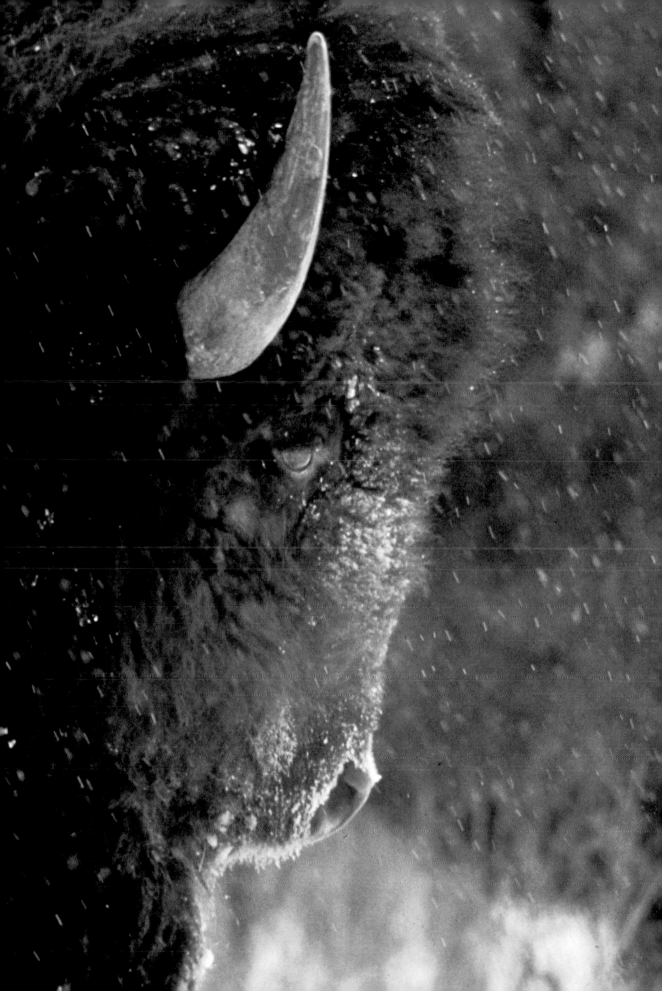

Above. *The Pawnee National Grasslands of northeastern Colorado are a rare remnant of the great prairies that once stretched over much of the American West.*

Left. Setaria *grasses, belonging to a genus of about 60 species, flower in Texas. Because the soil is so rich, most North American grasslands have been converted to agriculture.*

Overleaf. *A flock of sandhill cranes* (Grus canadensis) *takes flight in New Mexico. Sandhill cranes live in flocks except during the breeding season, when couples pair off for nesting. The principal habitat of this bird is prairie, especially near marshy areas.*

ranches and farms, number perhaps 30,000. While the huge herds are gone, the species is not in danger of extinction.

The Pronghorn

Once almost as numerous as the bison, the pronghorn (*Antilocapra americana*) feeds more selectively but can manage on more arid land. Although often called an "antelope," the pronghorn is only distantly related to the true antelopes of Africa and Asia. Evidence of this is the fact that the horn is sheathed in a covering of bone that falls off and is regenerated annually, in the manner of a deer's antler. This is not known to occur among true antelopes.

The fastest animal in the Western Hemisphere, the pronghorn can run at up to 95 kilometers an hour. When it is alarmed, its white rump flashes brilliantly in the sun. The pronghorn emits this "signal"—received by its fellows —by spreading the hairs on its rump. It can be seen for miles.

Like the bison, the pronghorn was almost exterminated, but it has been carefully managed in recent years. It now numbers in the hundreds of thousands, although some races are still rare, and it is gone from much of the country it formerly inhabited.

Because the pronghorn can live in drier areas than the bison, its range extended beyond that of the latter into the sagebrush plains and semi-desert, even to the Pacific Ocean in areas such as Baja California.

Prairie Dog Towns

Prairie dogs were once seen on prairies even more often than bisons and pronghorns. They are actually rodents but derive their name from the fact that, when alarmed, they bark like dogs. In the recent past, prairie dog colonies of millions of individuals were spread over the North American grasslands. These colonies, called prairie dog towns, contained thousands of entrances to networks of subterranean tunnels and chambers, as well as "streets" and paths which sometimes extended for miles between the holes. At each entrance, to prevent flooding of the underground tunnel system, a prairie dog builds a tight-packed earth threshold, which hardens and becomes a very stable dam.

Prairie dogs are diurnal: all their feeding takes place in the daytime. They do not venture far from their protective burrows and at the first sight of potential danger give a piercing whistle. All nearby individuals then rush to their burrows, either disappearing inside or waiting outside in an upright position to watch the intruder's movements. People are the prairie dog's greatest enemy; but they are also preyed on by coyotes (*Canis latrans*), badgers (*Taxidea taxus*), black-footed ferrets (*Mustela nigripes*), foxes (*Vulpes fulva*), and golden eagles (*Aquila chrysaetos*). Burrowing owls (*Speotyto cunicularia*), rattlesnakes, and long-tailed weasels (*Mustela frenata*) seize young prairie dogs in their nests or tunnels.

In the northern parts of their range prairie dogs keep to their underground burrows during the winter. However, theirs is not a true coma-like hibernation. During the preceding months they build up a fat layer that serves as

metabolic fuel during their passive period. One reason for the wide expansion of prairie dog colonies in the past may be the fact that rattlesnakes used their burrows for hibernation, forcing the rodents to move to other quarters.

The black-tailed prairie dog is still the most numerous species. Not long ago it occurred in enormous colonies on the plains and foothills from Saskatchewan to Arizona and Mexico. It preferred shortgrass prairies, which the bison and pronghorn provided. Farmers made war on the prairie dogs because the rodents competed with grazing livestock. Nowadays only colonies in reserves survive. Several predatory species, such as the black-footed ferret, coyote, and burrowing owl, which preyed on prairie dogs, have been hurt by their disappearance.

Other Rodents of the Prairie

At least one rodent remained abundant on the prairie despite poisoning, cultivation, cattle grazing, hunting, and motor traffic. Richardson's ground squirrel (*Spermophilus richardsoni*) still has a wide range on the Great Plains and has easily adapted to areas heavily grazed by livestock. Like so many of its relatives—there are 28 species of ground squirrels in North America—this ground squirrel lives in colonies in burrows, but each family keeps to itself within the community.

A few of the 22 other rodents common in various prairie areas are the prairie vole (*Microtus ochrogaster*), deer mouse (*Peromyscus maniculatus*), plains harvest mouse (*Reithrodontomys montanus*), and plains pocket gopher (*Geomys bursarius*). Muskrats (*Ondatra zibethica*) are common in almost all prairie marshes, where their conical houses are easy to observe in the water. Among the largest rodents of the plains are three species of cottontails (*Sylvilagus*) and two of jackrabbits, the white-tailed jackrabbit (*Lepus townsendi*) and black-tailed jackrabbit (*L. californicus*).

The biggest jackrabbit is the white-tailed, which may weigh 4.5 kilograms. The others are slightly smaller. All share the same type of gait, a short hop rather than a walk when casually moving, and a bounding run when in danger.

A jackrabbit on the move is a spectacular sight. It sometimes covers more than a dozen feet in a single jump. Ears raised, the creature speeds on, surmounting obstacles that may be shoulder-high to a man. Every so often, the rabbit zooms upward in the middle of a bound to catch sight of whatever is giving chase. At top speed, the animal may move at 70 kilometers an hour. Jackrabbits may be pursued by coyotes, domestic dogs, foxes, rattlesnakes, or eagles.

With huge ears, the jackrabbit, not surprisingly, has excellent hearing. It has a good sense of smell, too, and moderate vision. Usually silent, the rabbit screams fearfully when it is attacked.

Jackrabbits forage by night, when they are least likely to be seen. They are highly adaptable feeders, eating sage, cactus, a variety of shrubs, and especially grass. A jackrabbit usually keeps to a relatively small home range of a few square kilometers, but if drought eliminates its food supply, it may wander far in search of something to eat.

141

Ferrets and Other Carnivores

When whites settled on the prairies, several carnivores were wiped out by their traps, poison, and domestic dogs. In Canada, the last prairie grizzlies (*Ursus arctos*) were quickly exterminated; the black bear (*U. americanus*) was eliminated about 1900, and the wolf (*Canis lupus*) and the prairie fox or northern kit fox (*Vulpes velox hebes*) in 1920. The latter formerly ranged across the plains of western Canada and the United States but is now confined to the Cypress Hills of southwestern Saskatchewan and even there it is very rare.

The black-footed ferret may be the rarest mammal in the United States. Reaching about 60 centimeters in length, including the tail, the ferret weighs less than a kilogram, with females generally smaller. The legs of the ferret are short, and have large claws on the front paws adapted for digging. With a long, muscular body, the animal can squirm into very narrow tunnels.

This large weasel is a denizen of prairie dog towns, which provide it with prey and den sites. Hence, its former range coincided with that of the prairie dog.

Unknown to science until 1851, the ferret may never have been common. But it was not a truly rare animal until perhaps the 1950s, when there was an effort throughout western North America to eliminate prairie dogs, mostly by poison.

Scientists believe that ferrets usually kill prairie dogs underground by night, while the rodents are sleeping, but also attack them in the open. The ferrets kill by slashing the victim's throat or neck with razor-sharp teeth, which can dispatch a prairie dog in moments. Sometimes, however, the prairie dog prey fights back. One scientist who was studying ferrets witnessed such a clash when four prairie dogs on the surface were confronted by two ferrets emerging from a burrow. One prairie dog tried to nip one of the ferrets, which backed off. When the other ferret moved in on the prairie dog, the latter withdrew. Suddenly, the prairie dog charged the ferret, bowling it over. The ferret bolted back into the burrow. The prairie dog immediately began to cover the burrow with dirt. Prairie dogs habitually try to seal off burrows in which ferrets are lurking. The rodents dig up dirt with their front feet, then kick it backward into the burrow with their hind feet. When the opening of the burrow is filled, the prairie dog tamps down the dirt with nose and forehead. Some scientists have even noted that the ferrets make their homes in burrows with unusually wide openings, which are more difficult for the prairie dogs to seal.

Although sealed in, the ferret is really in no danger. It is itself an excellent digger. When excavating, the ferret works rump outward, holding the dirt against its chest with its front paws, and dragging it from the tunnel.

Lone Coyotes and Tough Badgers

Important predators on remaining areas of the tamed prairies are the coyote and badger. Despite extermination campaigns that have enjoyed official encouragement from states and counties, the coyote has held out, albeit in much reduced numbers.

The coyote's main food consists of small mammals, birds, reptiles, insects, fruit, berries, and carrion. In size and

Above. *In a low spot on a Nebraska grassland, which is drained by the Missouri river, grasses flower profusely.*

Opposite. *An old Indian proverb says that if there is to be a last animal living on earth, it will be the coyote* (Canis latrans). *The saying is testament to the cunning and adaptability of this creature. Coyotes, also known as "prairie wolves," are ubiquitous throughout the western grasslands, and despite years of persecution by stockmen, they thrive. They have spread east into woodlands, even to the Atlantic seaboard, and can sometimes be found within the municipal limits of large western cities such as Los Angeles.*

partly in behavior the coyote is intermediate between a wolf and a fox. Usually it hunts alone, looking, listening, sniffing, and digging for rodents and insects, but sometimes it pursues larger mammals and birds. When stalking pronghorns or deer, coyotes may form a team in which the members take turns chasing the prey until it is exhausted. Coyotes cannot overtake pronghorns, but instead of fleeing in a straight line, the pronghorns run in circles in order to remain in familiar home territory or in the vicinity of the parent herd. Thus, by cooperating with each other the coyotes can run them down.

Like many other mammals, coyotes clean their dens carefully even when they adopt the burrows of badgers, prairie spotted skunks (*Spilogale interrupta*), and foxes. These other animals also pay much attention to den sanitation. The badger even arranges a separate toilet area.

Chiefly an animal of the treeless plains, the badger feeds on rodents, reptiles, insects, and probably vegetables. It is not shy of people, but the rapidity with which it can dig itself beyond reach of teams of up to ten men is amazing. It is a very tough and courageous animal, able to defend itself even against several dogs, but its main defense in treeless country is escape by digging.

The badger is common on many prairies and may in some areas be encountered even by day, though it is mainly crepuscular and nocturnal. Its body is very flat and wide —much more so than that of the Eurasian badger. The burrows of the American species may extend from 2 to 3 meters below the surface. Dug by such a flat-shaped animal they are wider than they are high.

Dance of the Prairie Chicken

The greater prairie chicken (*Tympanuchus cupido pinnatus*) is a typical ground bird of North American grasslands. It is confined to remaining prairie habitats and other suitable localities from central southern Canada to northeastern Oklahoma, but it is everywhere rare and in most areas decreasing in numbers. Despite vanishing prairies, the greater prairie chicken may be saved if enough of its food plants are cultivated.

The prairie chicken's spring courtship display when the cocks boom and dance before the hens is a remarkable performance and greatly influenced Indian dances, costumes, and music. Every morning from March to May about half an hour before sunrise, the cocks begin to gather at certain dance grounds and immediately start performing, while other cocks fly in to join them. With bright orange-colored inflated air sacs on each side of the neck, head plumes spread out, wings drooping, and tail fanned out over the back, the birds strut around on the arena and emit beautiful hollow booms—a sound that can be heard for miles—by expelling the air from the sacs. As a solo performance this is impressive, but when a dozen or more cocks boom in a mighty chorus for hours, the scenic and vocal effect becomes overwhelming. The cocks pirouette and bow, circle about, threaten one another, or court the females that make discreet visits to the arena. Sometimes genuine battles between males take place, each one striking with bills and feet until the feathers fly. A southern race of the prairie chicken (*T. c. attwateri*) occurs, but only in a few areas in Texas.

Above, opposite. *The pronghorn* (Antilocapra americana) *is the fastest animal in North America. It can move at a speed of up to 95 kilometers an hour. Like the tail of the white-tailed deer, the pronghorn's white rump indicates that the animal is alarmed. A true grasslands creature, the pronghorn is able to survive on tough vegetation and little water. The pronghorn's name derives from its distinctive horn pattern, which is unlike that of any other living animal.*

Bobwhites and Other Prairie Birds

In contrast to the prairie chicken, the masked bobwhite (*Colinus virginianus ridgwayi*) seems always to have been limited to grasslands between southern Arizona and northwestern Mexico. The grazing and trampling of the grass by cattle has damaged its habitat so badly that it is now found in only a few localities.

Efforts are underway to reestablish populations of masked bobwhites from birds bred in captivity. Although conservationists have propagated a sufficient number of birds, the habitat that suits the masked bobwhite is at a premium. Known to science for only about a century, the masked bobwhite has very special habitat preferences. It apparently survives only in open savanna grassland, subtropical in nature, such as was once found in southern Arizona and Sonora, Mexico. Much of this grassland has been changed by grazing and human development.

Masked bobwhites—the name comes from the black color of the male's face—tend to live in very dense grass. This is especially true in nesting season, for the nest is placed on the ground. In fact, unless growth of grass provides sufficient cover, the birds will postpone breeding. The breeding season begins in early summer, peaking during August. As the season approaches, the birds, which have lived in coveys, begin to pair. A sign that the birds are pairing is the calling of the males, which begins in late June if the grass has grown tall enough to suit them. Interestingly, the male does not seem willing to call unless the temperature of the day has reached at least 13 degrees C. and the humidity 25 percent.

Young masked bobwhites hatch in early fall, with 5–15 offspring constituting the normal brood size. The young are capable of reproducing after a year.

Few other species demonstrate so graphically how excessive grazing and resultant destruction of grass by livestock can cause the decline of a grasslands animal. In the late 1800s, as the threat of raiding by Apache Indians receded, southern Arizona became the scene of increasingly intensive cattle ranching. Favored areas for cattle were the grassy river bottoms and other pastures that the bobwhite also preferred. By the beginning of this century, the bobwhite had disappeared from Arizona, although it held out in adjacent Sonora, where the livestock industry was less developed.

As the decades passed, ranching increased in Sonora as well, and the birds declined there, too. Grasslands in Sonora, once lush, have been stripped, and there are few signs that the trend will be reversed. Birds captured in Sonora, however, have been propagated by federal agencies. Some masked bobwhites have now been reintroduced in a few protected areas in southern Arizona. The birds appear to be flourishing. If more such areas can be set aside, the species may replenish itself.

Fortunately, many prairie birds have been able to adapt to cultivation of their old grassy habitats. The western meadowlark (*Sturnella neglecta*) and the very similar eastern meadowlark (*S. magna*) are common in open grassy fields of eastern North America. Although these two closely related species look like twins, they have very different songs and calls. Among other passerines on the prairie are the bobolink (*Dolichonyx oryzivorus*), Sprague's pipit (*Anthus spragueii*), horned lark

(*Eremophila alpestris*), lark bunting (*Calamospiza melanocorys*), sparrows of several genera, and longspurs (*Calcarius*). The prairie warbler (*Dendroica discolor*) has expanded rapidly and successfully during the last 150 years, perhaps because males make routine explorations of areas surrounding their territories.

Of the raptors, only the prairie falcon (*Falco americanus*) is peculiar to prairie habitats; it has a restricted distribution in southwestern Canada and the northwestern United States. Almost as large as a peregrine (*F. peregrinus*), it feeds on birds of various sizes from prairie chickens and doves to horned larks and on mammals like gophers, ground squirrels, voles, and mice as well as insects.

The prairie falcon has a brown back. Below it is white with dark markings. Its high-pitched scream has been likened to a puppy's bark.

During breeding season, the female falcon often deposits its 3–6 eggs in old raven nests, or may place them on bare rock or in a crevice. The eggs are incubated for about a month, usually by the female.

Another bird of prey with a range almost exclusively in the prairies is the ferruginous hawk (*Buteo regalis*). This hawk has a wingspan of 1.4 meters and tends to soar high in the air while looking for prey. Its principal victims are mice, ground squirrels, and similar mammals, although sometimes it will eat large insects.

High above the western grasslands, the impressive golden eagle is not an unfamiliar sight. The red-tailed hawk (*Buteo jamaicensis*) is also common.

In western Canada, the plains are dotted with marshes, lakes, and ponds with an extremely rich bird fauna; in spring and summer, bird calls, colors, and displays fill some of these prairies. Red-winged blackbirds (*Agelaius phoeniceus*) nest in almost every pond with reeds, cattail and bullrushes. The greatest number of waterfowl are found around potholes and marshes.

The prairie pothole region makes up only 10 percent of North America's total waterfowl breeding area, but it produces 50 percent of the continent's ducks in an average year and more in particularly abundant years.

Rattlesnakes, Bull Snakes, and Blue Racers
The three most prominent reptiles of the prairies are the prairie rattlesnake, bull snake (*Pituophis sayi*), and blue racer (*Coluber constrictor*). The prairie rattlesnake, which may reach a length of 1.5 meters, uses prairie dog dens as winter refuges. The bull snake, one of the largest snakes in North America, can grow up to 2.4 meters long. Like the prairie rattlesnake, it is an efficient predator of rodents; it kills larger prey by constriction and swallows smaller ones directly. The blue racer is also a large snake, more than 1.5 meters long. Unlike most snakes, it moves with its head raised well above the ground. Around ponds and marshes common garter snakes (*Thamnophis sirtalis*) and western garter snakes (*T. ordinoides*) are abundant.

Mammals of Sagebrush Country
The sagebrush country of the Great Basin and other grasslands west of the true prairies has been somewhat spared the environmental destruction that has overtaken habitats east of the Rocky Mountains. By the time human

Above. *A Richardson's ground squirrel* (Spermophilus richardsoni) *chatters away. Small ground squirrels—this one would fit in one's hand—remain numerous in the American West because, unlike many other creatures, they can survive in areas that have been grazed down by cattle.*

Opposite. *A white-tailed jackrabbit* (Lepus townsendi) *crouches low on the North American plains. Its droopy ears indicate that it is resting undisturbed. Largest of jackrabbits, this species inhabits northern plains.*

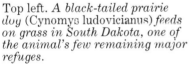

Top left. *A black-tailed prairie dog* (Cynomys ludovicianus) *feeds on grass in South Dakota, one of the animal's few remaining major refuges.*

Center. *A prairie dog scratches in an attempt to rid itself of fleas. Prairie dogs live in colonies, called "towns," which may be inhabited by thousands of individuals. Even today one can see, in a few places, towns that stretch from horizon to horizon.*

Right. *The prairie dog gets its name from its barking call. Living in burrows, each surmounted by a large mound, prairie dogs emerge by day to feed. If alarmed—say, by a hawk soaring overhead—the creatures dive back into the shelter of their burrows.*

Bottom. *An adult black-tailed prairie dog nuzzles a youngster in a gesture of recognition common to the animals. Young black-tails stay in the burrow for the first six weeks of their lives. Only then do they venture out.*

settlement of the far western grasslands had become intense, the move to set aside national parks was underway. Some of the western grasslands therefore resemble true wildernesses.

In a natural state, sagebrush grows mixed with grasses. It may invade areas where overgrazing by domestic stock has reduced the grasses. Because sagebrush is not palatable to livestock, domestic herds may avoid such invaded regions. Grasses may recover amidst the sagebrush, and if not disturbed such areas can become good grasslands wildlife habitat again.

Many prairie animals such as the pronghorn, which can, if need be, eat sagebrush, inhabit land dominated by this shrub. The most common larger animal of sagebrush, however, is the mule deer (*Odocoileus hemionus*). This deer regularly weighs over 90 kilograms and has very large ears, which explains its common name.

In summer mule deer usually segregate, forming smaller groups of two or three animals, or appearing singly. After the mating season, which occurs in November and December, the deer associate in larger herds. When alarmed, it runs with a strange high-bounding gait, leaping and landing on all four feet simultaneously. On the flat plains this form of locomotion is obviously not very efficient, and it may have evolved in other habitats to which the species is better adapted.

During the warm months, the mule deer goes high into mountains, which often rise near the grasslands, to take advantage of the high-altitude summer pastures. Winter brings it down to the grasslands again, where the food supply survives the cold period. The mule deer depends heavily on grasses, but also if need be browses on shrubs and small trees, including oak, cedar, fir, and jack pine (*Pinus banksiana*).

Young mule deer are born in early summer after a gestation of about 210 days. At birth, a fawn weighs about 2.5 kilograms. Once able to walk, the young mule deer is hidden by the mother, which then feeds some distance away to conceal the location of the fawn.

In the days when the wolf still roved the grasslands, it was an important enemy of the mule deer.

Sagebrush Birds

Many North American prairie birds, including the horned lark, burrowing owl, and prairie falcon, also occur in sagebrush country, but a few species appear to be most at home in this habitat, namely Brewer's sparrow (*Spizella breweri*), sage sparrow (*Amphispiza belli*), green-tailed towhee (*Chlorura chlorura*), sage thrasher (*Oreoscoptes montanus*), poor-will (*Caprimulgus vociferus*), and sage grouse (*Centrocercus urophasianus*).

One of the most interesting of these is the sage grouse. It is the largest American grouse and has a long tail almost like that of a pheasant. The cock's courting display in spring is even more remarkable than that of the prairie chicken. The males gather in the darkness before dawn at certain traditional arenas. There the male spreads his tail feathers like a fan and bends them over his back. He then inflates the large air sacs on the breast and sides of the neck so that they reach almost to the ground. The sacs are pumped rapidly up and down, while the stiffened feathers on the neck and breast rasp against each other and against

Overleaf. With mouths agape, three young horned larks (Eremophila alpestris) wait for food. Found in Eurasia, North Africa, and the Americas, the horned lark is truly a bird of open country and is very abundant on the North American prairies.

Above. Young ferruginous hawks remain in the nest for two months after birth. Nests may be constructed on the ground, a stump, a rocky outcrop, or in a tree.

Opposite. In a ground nest, young ferruginous hawks (Buteo regalis) await food from their parents. These hawks feed almost solely on rodents.

the wings, producing a rattling sound. In this posture the male bows to the ground and emits a sonorous cry which is intensified by the air sacs.

Reptiles, Amphibians, and Insects
The prairie rattlesnake and bull snake also live in sagebrush habitats. A nocturnal and little-known species is the long-nosed snake (*Rhinocheilus lecontei*), probably a burrower. The striped whip snake (*Coluber taeniatus*), a diurnal reptile, hunts insects, birds, and rodents. Lizards are common here: the sagebrush lizard (*Sceloporus graciosus*) and collared lizard (*Crotaphytus collaris*) are seen much more often than snakes. Amphibians include the western toad (*Bufo boreas*) and western spadefoot (*Scaphiosus hammondi*). Harvester ants (*Pogonomyrmex occidentalis*) and honey ants (*Myrmecocystus mexicanus*) build conspicuous mounds—a typical part of the sagebrush community.

Mesquite Grasslands
Dry grasslands of triple-awned grass (*Aristida*) and grama grass (*Bouteloua*) with several species of mesquite (*Prosopis*)—a spiny tree or bush with bean-like pods—dominate southern Arizona, southeastern Texas, and northern Mexico. Cacti such as the prickly pear (*Opuntia ficus indica*) and the creosote bush (*Larrea divaricata*) also occur. These areas come close to semi-desert and may form very arid habitats. Many areas exhibit various transitional vegetation stages, with the grasslands of yesterday on the way to becoming the deserts of tomorrow. Some scientists believe that North American deserts such as the Sonoran and Chihuahuan used to be grasslands but were transformed by man.

Around ten o'clock on any July morning in a region such as that near San Antonio in southern Texas, mesquite habitats appear as lifeless as deserts. The vertebrate populations are all hiding in the shade or have gone underground. One of the few exceptions is an amphibian, the green tree frog (*Hyla cinerea*). Unaffected by the shimmering heat, it sits on the shaded side of reed stems. All night until about nine in the morning, mesquite habitats are very much alive with animals. Even this dry and hot region has a well-developed fauna. Among mammals, rodents dominate. Several species such as the deer mouse, little pocket mouse (*Perognathus longimembris*) and black-tailed jackrabbit, also occur in the sagebrush communities. Rodent species typical of mesquite and other semiarid habitats are the southern grasshopper mouse (*Onychomys torridus*), cactus mouse (*Peromyscus eremicus*), Merriam kangaroo rat (*Dipodomys merriami*), rock pocket mouse (*Perognathus intermedius*), round-tailed ground squirrel (*Spermophilus tereticaudus*), spotted ground squirrel (*S. spilosomus*) and desert cottontail (*Sylvilagus auduboni*). The last-named has a wide range in the semiarid and arid Southwest, preferring valleys where the vegetation is most concentrated. Pocket mice store seeds in cheek pouches that can be stretched to hold considerable quantities. At night, these mice carry food to underground storehouses connected to their burrows.

The collared peccary (*Tayassu tajacu*), an active relative of the pig—but not a true swine—can be seen in the

*The western hog-nosed snake (*Heterodon nasicus*) is found on prairies and in semi-desert areas. Like its eastern counterpart, it feeds on toads. It is named for its upturned nose, with which it probes for toads in sandy soil.*

Left. *When frightened, the hog-nosed snake is a magnificent bluffer. It first puffs up the forward portion of its body, spreading its head and neck, while hissing air and pretending to strike. If this tactic fails to turn away an enemy, the snake turns over on its back and plays dead. If the snake is righted, it will simply flip over again and continue its act.*

Overleaf. *A marsh hawk (Circus cyaneus) feeds on the intestine of a rabbit. These birds hunt by flying low over grasses, alert for rodents, birds, reptiles, and other small creatures. Marsh hawks inhabit North America, Eurasia, the West Indies, northern South America, and North Africa as a breeding and wintering bird.*

159

The male sage grouse
(Centrocercus urophasianus) *has
an impressive mating ritual.
Cocks strut about one another in
a "threat" display. During the
performance, the males utter
booming calls, spread their tail
feathers, and inflate the twin sacs
on their breasts. These sacs
balloon into great yellow bags
that are visible up to 300 meters
away. The frequency of display
depends on a specific male's rank
within the hierarchy of cocks in
the vicinity. The dominant male
engages in almost three fourths of
all matings.*

mesquite grasslands and scrub from the border country of the southwestern United States southward. About 60 centimeters high at the shoulder, and weighing no more than 30 kilograms, the peccary runs in herds of a few to several dozen animals. Quick on its feet, it has tusk-like canine teeth, which can inflict severe injuries on its opponents. The enemies of the peccary are the large cats, such as the cougar and, especially in the south, the jaguar (*Felis onca*). Smaller predators, such as a bobcat (*Lynx rufus*) or coyote, may take a young peccary, but would be outmatched by an adult, and cut to ribbons by a herd.

Normally, a peccary herd scatters and runs when threatened, but these animals can fight ferociously. A peccary kills snakes by stomping on them with its very sharp hooves. Peccaries eat a wide variety of items, including snakes, lizards, bird eggs, fruits, acorns, roots, and the fruit of the prickly pear cactus, including the spines.

Birds in the Mesquite
The bird fauna of the mesquite is richer in species and numbers than the pure sagebrush communities, partly because many birds of South American origin penetrate Arizona, Texas, and northern Mexico. Some sagebrush birds, such as the black-throated sparrow (*Amphispiza bilineata*) and great horned owl (*Bubo virginianus*), inhabit the mesquite as well. But quite a high number of species are principally found in mesquite country. Among these are the curve-billed thrasher (*Toxostoma curvirostre*) and roadrunner (*Geococcyx californianus*). One mesquite bird, the red-tailed hawk, ranges over almost all of North America. In mesquite country, mice and other rodents are its staple food. It watches the movements of these small mammals either from a tree or from the air, announcing its presence with high-pitched calls. The cactus wren (*Campylorhynchus brunneicapillus*) is a giant compared to other wrens. It thrives in mesquite thickets but has also adapted to cultivated areas. For some reason, the males build numerous nests—perhaps as decoys—while the female is incubating in the real nest.

A Reptile Stronghold
Species of reptiles are more numerous in mesquite habitats than in other North American grasslands. Several also occur in sagebrush and desert communities. When disturbed, the western diamondback rattlesnake (*Crotalox atrox*) usually forms a coil and gives warning by rattling its tail persistently. The rattle at the end of the tail consists of interlocking horny segments which are re-formed each time the snake sheds its skin. Thus at birth the rattlesnake has no rattle, only a horny knob. The rattle varies with the speed of vibration, which in turn reflects the degree of the snake's excitement.

The diamondback is sometimes more than 2 meters long. This snake—like all rattlers—belongs to a group called "pit vipers." The name comes from the pit-like structure, one behind each eye, that permits the snake to sense the heat given off by the bodies of the warm-blooded animals, such as rodents, which are its prey. Tiny nerves in the pit can pick up one three-thousandth of a degree C. from

Left, overleaf. *The greater prairie chicken* (Tympanuchus cupido), *related to the grouse, also displays in a spectacular fashion during mating season. Males gather on the display—or "booming"—ground to perform and to carry on ritual combat in front of the females. The males inflate yellow sacs, raise spiked feathers on the sides of their necks, and make booming sounds. Females visit the periphery of the display area, where mating may take place.*

Above. *A regal fritillary (Speyeria idalia) alights on a thistle (Cirsium). The largest North American fritillary, this species is a prairie specialist that is becoming rare due to the reduction of its habitat.*

Opposite. *A crab spider (Thomisidae) perches on the head of a black sampson, or purple coneflower (Echinacea angustifolia). Here the spider waits to capture bees, flies, and other insects that visit the flower.*

almost a meter away. With this organ the rattlesnake can locate creatures such as mice and rats at night, its normal hunting time.

Among the most advanced snakes from the point of view of evolution, the pit vipers have fangs that are remarkably efficient for injecting venom into a victim. Very long, and needle sharp, they resemble slightly curved hypodermic needles, in that within each fang is a channel through which venom is pumped into the target.

Much has been made of the speed with which a rattlesnake strikes. However, experiments with a western diamondback show that this has been exaggerated. The diamondback under observation moved at 5.4 meters per second, much slower, for instance, than the left jab of a professional prizefighter.

Of the 15 species of rattlesnakes in North America, a dozen are found in the southwestern United States, including the region of mesquite and sagebrush grassland. Among them are the tiger rattler (*Crotalus tigris*) and the western diamond rattlesnake. The latter and the prairie rattlesnake are grasslands species, ranging far beyond the Southwest through much of the prairie region.

Some other snakes seem to mimic the rattler's habit of rattling its tail. Among them is the small leaf-nosed snake (*Phyllorhynchus decurtatus*), only 38 centimeters long, which inhabits the mesquite grassland. When it vibrates its tail in dead vegetation, the sound is very much like the buzz of a rattlesnake. Secretive, the leaf-nosed snake burrows in the sand, where it hunts small lizards. It is harmless to man.

Among lizards, the tree uta (*Uta ornata*) of Texas has developed tail scales which protrude like hooks and facilitate tree climbing. Spiny lizards (*Sceloporus*) of several species are common. Other lizards include the zebra-tailed lizard (*Callisaurus draconoides*), chuckwalla (*Sauromalus obesus*), crested lizard (*Dipsosaurus dorsalis*), and banded gecko (*Coleonyx variegatus*). The chuckwalla is a large herbivorous lizard that must take its time in eating. It is therefore usually active in the mornings before it gets too hot.

Other reptiles, such as the western gopher turtle or tortoise (*Gopherus agassizi*) and Berlandier's tortoise (*G. berlandieri*), are threatened by illegal collecting, trading, and exploitation as pets despite the fact that they usually do not survive outside their natural habitat.

Future of the Grasslands

In their natural state, the great grasslands of North America were the most productive area, in terms of animals, of the Northern Hemisphere and of the temperate regions of the world. This animal resource was wiped out only a century ago. Despite cultivation and soil erosion these grasslands became the breadbasket of the world. Now the remaining prairies may be exploited for their deposits of coal—another grave menace to the wildlife of the grasslands.

Llanos, Campos, and Pampas of South America

South America has vast, windblown steppes, expanses of semiarid bush, and a variety of savannas. Although these grasslands lack most of the larger animals typical of similar landscapes elsewhere, they are the home of creatures so unusual that they compensate for the lack of big animal spectacles. Many of these animals are found in more than one grassland zone. By and large the savannas of different types share the same groups of animals.

The Flooded Savanna

Two types of tropical and subtropical savanna, known as llanos, are temporarily flooded each year. One type is characterized by bunchgrass with scattered trees, the other by tallgrasses, especially the species *Paspalum fasciculatum*.

Generally bordered by dry, deciduous forests, intersected by countless rivers, surrounded by gallery forests, and broken by numerous marshes, llanos and similar habitats can be found in Colombia, Bolivia, Brazil, Paraguay, and Argentina. The largest areas are in the Orinoco river basin of Guyana and Venezuela. There the seasonal nature of the floods and their impact are very evident.

By April, when the dry season ends, the llano is arid and baked by the sun. Fires sweep through the region, particularly in the driest portions. Here, because of a resistance to fire, grows the llano palm (*Copernicia tectorum*), both individually and in groves. In the heart of the llano there are also thickets of trees such as the cassias (*Cassia aculeata*) and araguaney (*Tabebuia chrysantha*), the national tree of Venezuela.

Before the end of April, the rains come, and the llanos change dramatically, becoming vast floodplains dotted with lakes, lagoons, and marshes. The region will remain in this stage until October.

Because of the flooding, aquatic species are among the more characteristic animals of the llano. One of the most remarkable of these is the capybara (*Hydrochoerus hydrochaeris*), a water-loving creature that, weighing up to 65.5 kilograms, is the world's largest rodent.

The capybara feeds both on land and in water, grazing on various grasses and consuming aquatic herbs. Social animals living in large groups, capybaras are quite noisy. They are sedentary but they must move as water levels change in order to have land habitats for grazing and resting. They make a habit of basking on riverbanks. When threatened they plunge into the water.

Capybaras often feed or rest in waters completely covered by water hyacinths; only their heads and backs protrude above the plant surface. Birds perch on the backs of the capybaras and the water birds called jacanas (*Jacana spinosa*) sometimes trot over the rodents. Many of the capybara's activities, including copulation, take place in the water. The young reach sexual maturity at about one year. Humans and dogs are the prime enemies of the capybara, but in the llano, caimans (*Caiman crocodilus*), Orinoco crocodiles (*Crocodilus intermedius*), and anacondas (*Eunectes murinus*) also prey on them in the water, while cougars (*Felis concolor*), crab-eating foxes (*Cerdocyon thous*), and boas (*Constrictor constrictor*) pursue them on land.

Two small species of deer, the white-tailed (*Odocoileus virginianus gymnotis*) and red brocket (*Mazama*

173

Above. *Anthills dot the open grasslands of the Xingú region of the southern Mato Grosso.*

americana), also inhabit the llano. Both species, and especially the red brocket, are chiefly forest dwellers but often visit neighboring grasslands. An excellent swimmer, able to cross wide expanses of water, the red brocket is well adapted to the flooded llano. These two deer are the only wild hoofed animals of the immense llano, in sharp contrast to the life on the grasslands of Africa and Asia.

Anteaters, Armadillos, and Sloths

South American savannas have representatives of an animal group not found on grasslands of the Old World, the edentates (Edentata)—anteaters, armadillos, and sloths. On the llano, the edentate representatives are the giant anteater (*Myrmecophaga tridactyla*) and the giant armadillo (*Priodontes giganteus*). The anteater fills approximately the same ecological niche as the aardvark on the grasslands of Africa, even though the two species belong to different orders. Both species are proficient at opening concrete-hard termite nests and using their sticky tongues to capture tiny insects as well as ants. The giant anteater has developed a remarkably elongated head with a tubular snout and mouth. It has no teeth but has a very long tongue and strong, sharp claws on the forelegs. These tools enable it to reach its special food and also to inflict severe wounds. The tail of the giant anteater is long and bushy but is usually hairless in captivity.

The giant armadillo, weighing 45 kilograms, is also equipped with enormous foreclaws. The third front digit is particularly well developed and is used as a tool for slashing termite hills and as a spade for digging into the earth. While the anteater is toothless, the giant armadillo has more teeth than any other terrestrial mammal, but they are small and rootless—probably a heritage from the past when their even larger forefathers had some use for teeth. All armadillos are protected by a remarkable armor consisting of overlapping shield-like plates which also cover the head and tail. The band-like segments of this armor are movable and some species are able to roll themselves into a ball for defense. The giant armadillo and other armadillos are survivors of an order that in the Pliocene and Pleistocene epochs was a prominent part of South American fauna.

Water Birds of the Llanos

Probably no other area in the world has so many species of herons, as well as storks and ibises, as the Venezuelan llano. Many of these, such as the scarlet ibis (*Eudocimus ruber*), roseate spoonbill (*Ajaia ajaja*), and agami heron (*Agamia agami*), are very colorful. The last is so unusual that it is placed in a genus of its own. The plumage of the adult bird is brilliant chestnut, iridescent green-blue and pale blue or gray. The legs are yellow and the spear-like, sky-blue bill is of a different shape from that of other herons; it may well be an isolated offshoot from an ancient group of herons. On the llanos, one also finds the American flamingo (*Phoenicopterus ruber*).

In the riverine thickets is an avian surprise, the hoatzin (*Opisthocomus hoazin*), a bizarre crested bird, which may be a descendant of *Archaeopteryx*, a prehistoric link between reptiles and birds. Like young hoatzins, adult *Archaeopteryx* had claws on the wings, which is only one of the anatomical and behavioral peculiarities that has led

177 top. *A mother pampas deer* (Ozotoceros bezoarticus) *greets her fawn. If her fawn is threatened, the mother may try to lead the enemy away by feigning an injured leg. This species ranges dry grasslands from Brazil to Patagonia.*

Center. *The maned wolf* (Chrysocyon brachyurus) *of the pampas is a shy animal. It preys on pacas* (Cuniculus), *agoutis* (Dasyprocta), *birds, reptiles, and insects. It also eats fruit.*

Bottom. *A pregnant puma* (Felis concolor) *rests in the grass of Goiás State, Brazil. Although their range has decreased somewhat, pumas are still widespread in South America. They are more likely to be found in drier, open areas than in wet forest.*

Overleaf. *The six-banded armadillo* (Euphractus sexcinctus) *ranges grasslands east of the Andes throughout most of South America. Weighing 4 to 5 kilograms, the armadillo is very feisty. It fights enemies with teeth and large claws; it also uses the claws for digging burrows.*

scientists to place this bird in an order by itself. Newly hatched hoatzins are equipped with three functional claws on each wing. Within a few days after hatching the nestlings begin to climb in the trees, using the wing claws and the feet to grasp branches and twigs. After three or four weeks the claws are dropped. The nesting tree often stands in a flooded area and another unusual characteristic in young hoatzins is their ability to swim if they fall into the water below. When they reach the tree trunk, the young birds just climb back to the nest.

Huge and Venomous Snakes

During floodtime some reptiles greatly increase their range on the savanna. The anaconda occurs along the rivers of the llano. No other giant serpent spends so much time in water and it is often seen partly submerged or floating with only the nostrils and eyes above the surface. This snake, the largest in the New World, is generally about 6 meters long. There have been reports of giants more than 20 meters long but the largest officially recorded is 11.3 meters.

In unflooded areas of the savanna lives another large snake, the boa, which prefers clumps of trees or bushes and gallery forests. Other conspicuous reptiles are the tropical rattler (*Crotalus durissimus*), green iguana (*Iguana iguana*), and tegu (*Tupinambis teguixin*); the two latter, the largest lizards in South America, reach a length of as much as 1.5 meters.

The Montes, Campos, and Caatingas

Wide areas of Brazil, Paraguay, Uruguay, Argentina, and Bolivia support drier savannas or arid brushlands, or dry woodlands and forests. Depending on their character, these areas are called montes, campos, or caatingas. Although patchy in distribution, the montes and campos cover more of South America than any other type of tropical grasslands and include a wide range of habitats, from temporarily flooded grasslands similar to llanos to very dry steppe-like areas. Some campos remain underwater much of the year; some are treeless expanses; and others are patched with woods and jungle-like forests. Many campos penetrate into rain forests, while some are entirely isolated within a forest. The Mato Grosso in Brazil and the Gran Chaco in Argentina and Paraguay are essentially campo savannas or brushlands, but the proximity of the former to the Amazon rain forests and the latter to the Andean slopes influences them greatly. The Gran Chaco, for example, is mostly an extremely hot semi-desert where winds whirl up clouds of dust. Only cacti, which grow from 6 to 9 meters high, and xerophilous trees, up to 18 meters, seem to survive. But the grasses come back with the rains: in summer the area is transformed into an immense, mosquito-infested swamp, flooded by rains and swollen streams from the melting snows of the Andes and the cloud forests. Such regularly flooded lands are called *pantanal*.

Savannas with a very pronounced dry season, known as *campos cerrados*, occupy much of the Brazilian plateaus. In southeastern Brazil's Rio Grande do Sul, the savannas are lush and much like the llanos of Venezuela.

The caatingas occupy areas inside as well as outside the rain forest region. There are both evergreen caatingas

Above. *The crested tinamou* (Eudromia elegans) *is found in Argentina and Chile. The male incubates the eggs and rears the chicks. Nests are constructed on the ground, in grass, or in a bush.*

Opposite. *The greater rhea* (Rhea americana) *has habits much like those of the ostrich; however, the two birds may not be closely related. Male rheas tend the young, as do male ostriches. Rheas feed on leaves, seeds, and other plant material, as well as insects and small reptiles.*

Above. *Like the secretary bird of Africa, the crested seriema* (Cariama cristata) *feeds on snakes as well as insects. This bird of the pampas prefers to move on the ground rather than fly.*

Opposite. *The small burrowing owl* (Speotyto cunicularia) *ranges open country from Florida and western North America to Argentina. It usually nests in the abandoned burrows of rodents and similar animals, although it sometimes digs its own hole. Often these owls live in colonies.*

and deciduous caatingas. In the former, the soil is poor in nutrients and deficient in water, while the latter have a relatively rich soil and a climate of severe dry seasons where evaporation and transpiration exceed precipitation. A thorny vegetation of shrubs and cacti characterizes many caatingas. Vertebrate animals have adapted to these various types of grassy habitats where the vegetation may be pure grasslands and woodland savannas or thorny thickets and arid cactus country. Several llano animals—the capybara, giant anteater, and giant armadillo—also live on the more southerly grasslands.

Three armadillos show a pronounced decline, perhaps caused by the gradual cultivation of their habitats as well as by hunters. One is the greater pichiciego (*Burmeisteria retusa*) in the Chaco region; a second is the lesser pichiciego (*Chlamyphorus truncatus*) in central Argentina; and a third is the Brazilian three-banded armadillo (*Tolypeutes tricinctus*) in northeastern Brazil. These smaller armadillos are to a large extent subterranean, digging tunnel systems and generally visiting the surface at night. They feed mostly on roots but probably also consume insects. Due to its wide range, the best-known armadillo is the nine-banded (*Dasypus novemcinctus*). Though it occurs in grasslands and plains south to Gran Chaco, it is essentially a forest animal. Armadillos of the genus *Tolypeutes* roll up like an armored ball to defend themselves.

Southern Deer, Peccaries, and Wild Dogs

The southern savannas are richer in ungulates than the northern llanos. The South American swamp deer (*Blastocerus dichotomus*), the continent's largest deer, lives in swamps, wet grasslands, and temporarily inundated woodland savannas. Local inhabitants hunt it intensively because they value it highly as food and prepare medicines and aphrodisiacs from its antlers.

There are also two species of herd-living peccaries, the collared peccary and white-lipped peccary (*Tayassu albirostris*). Though they are mainly nocturnal, both are active by day. They are omnivorous and constantly on the move, roaming over large areas and swimming across rivers. Their prime habitat is the forest. Peccaries are gregarious, traveling in small bands, and they may be aggressive when wounded or cornered. These pigs have a large scent gland, located in the middle of the back, which produces a strong odor. Its function may be to facilitate contacts between members of a herd which in high grass or other vegetation do not always see each other. The peccaries appear to be fond of this odor, for they often rub each other's gland areas.

One of the more common mammals of the campos is the maned wolf (*Chrysocyon brachyurus*), a slender animal with long, almost stilt-like legs. Its numbers seem to be diminishing rapidly, but it is still found in parts of Brazil, eastern and northern Bolivia, Paraguay, and northern Argentina. It hunts at night and is able to run very fast, but has hardly any prey available other than rodents, birds, and insects. It also feeds on fruits to such an extent that Brazilians call those of one shrub, *Solanum grandiflorum*, the "maned wolf fruit."

Above. *A mantis (Mantidae)
stalks its prey. This fierce insect
hunts a variety of prey; large
mantids even eat young birds and
frogs. Once a victim is in range,
the mantis moves like lightning,
catching its prey between its front
legs in a twentieth of a second.*

Right. *This assassin bug
(Reduviidae) is laying its eggs. A
fierce little creature, it preys on
other insects. Some types of
assassin bugs can bite hard
enough to hurt humans.*

markets in North America and Europe—is valued highly. For that reason it has been hunted to extermination in its native haunts, but it is hoped that the nutria farms in North America, Europe, and Asia will ease the pressure on South America's wild populations. Coypus live in colonies within collective territories and build extensive tunnel systems in riverbanks.

Opossums, Cats, and Other Carnivores
Like all South American grasslands, the pampas are inhabited by opossums (Didelphidae). Though the majority prefer forests and woods, many species are common at the edges of forests, from which they visit the savannas. Some species even appear to be true grassland dwellers. One, a tiny mouse opossum (*Marmosa elegans*), is a marsupial but has no pouch. The young attach themselves firmly to the nipples of their mother and hang on while she is moving around.

Two cats still rove the pampas—the pampas cat (*Felis colocolo*) and kodkod (*F. guigna*). The former is medium-sized, 120–130 centimeters long, with a tail 30 centimeters long. It is a beautiful animal with long-haired, silver-gray fur marked by rust-brown stripes along upper parts of the body and spots on the sides—an unusual pelage for a cat.

Other carnivores are the Argentine skunk (*Conepatus chinga*), Patagonian weasel (*Lyncodon patagonicus*), pampas fox (*Dusicyon gymnocercus*), and Argentine fox (*D. griseus*). The skunk feeds chiefly on insects, the others on rodents. The weasel is the commonest carnivore of the pampas, but since it is nocturnal the gauchos, or cowboys, do not seem to be aware of its presence and abundance. Its diet is mainly rodents.

Pampas Birds
The burrowing owl, which is very widely distributed in South and North America, takes over viscacha holes on the pampas as it does the prairie dog holes in North American prairies. It can also dig its own burrows. One of the few owls that inhabit treeless plains, this species is active both day and night. By day it usually sits outside the entrance hole of its burrow. The underground tunnels can be as long as 3 meters and lead to a breeding chamber where the eggs are laid and the young reared. At dawn and dusk this owl hunts chiefly insects, but occasionally preys on small rodents and birds.

The pampas is also the breeding habitat of a parrot, the monk parakeet (*Myiopsittacus monachus*), which nests in colonies in trees. It constructs enormous nests in which each pair has its own compartment. The most characteristic wader of the moist parts of the pampas is the pampas plover (*Belonopterus cayennensis*), which seems to feed mainly on earthworms. Among the birds seen for several months every year are migratory waders from both the Northern and Southern Hemispheres. From North America come the American golden plover (*Pluvialis dominica dominica*), the godwit (*Limosa haemastica*), and several sandpipers (*Tringa* and *Calidris*). The golden plover makes the most remarkable migration. In the fall it leaves its nesting area in northernmost Alaska and Canada as well as in northern Siberia. The main part of the North American population

moves east and southeast across Canada to Labrador, Nova Scotia, and New England, then south over the Atlantic to spend the winter in southern Brazil and Argentina. Its spring movement takes it on a westerly path over the Amazon, the Isthmus of Panama or the Gulf of Mexico, the Mississippi Valley, and the Canadian prairies west of Hudson Bay. The golden plover then spreads to the west and east across its Arctic breeding grounds. The total distance of this long loop movement is about 25,600 kilometers! The explanation of this pattern seems to be both nutritional and ecological. In the fall the golden plover finds abundant nourishment on the Canadian tundra and along the North Atlantic coast before it flies over the Atlantic, but during the spring migration that coast is a frozen, snowbound land with dense fog, while the western route over Panama, Mexico, and the Mississippi Valley is hospitably warm and rich in nourishment.

The Steppes of Patagonia

The southern parts of the pampas merge gradually into the northern steppes of Patagonia. In Argentine Patagonia, pampas, steppes, and semi-deserts are the main vegetation habitats. Large areas of Patagonia consist of potential pampas, once rich grasslands where unwise or careless cultivation has led to a serious degradation of the soil.

Patagonia lies nearer to Antarctica than any other continental area. Because the Andes block off the Pacific rains from Patagonia, humidity decreases gradually from west to east, resulting in a very arid eastern plain. Patagonia's grasslands consist mainly of scrubs, grasses of bent (*Agrostis*), tussock (*Poa*), and sedges (*Carex*). Many animals of the pampas occur also on the Patagonian steppes. The herds of guanacos which once roamed both the Patagonian pampas and steppes have been greatly reduced, so that nowadays the animal is found mainly in the Andean highlands. There are few mammals on the Patagonian steppes aside from the mara and such other rodents as the tuco-tuco, here represented by *Ctenomys magellanicus*, a guinea pig or cavy (*Microcavia australis*), a rice rat (*Oryzomys longicaudatus magellanicus*), and a chinchilla (*Euneomys dabbeni*).

Among the birds of this area, the Magellan goose (*Chloephaga picta*) is notable. The male is larger than the female and is mostly white, whereas the female is dark brown, sometimes with a red tinge. This color difference between the sexes is unusual among geese. The goose breeds on the southern grasslands, wintering 1900 kilometers north in the valley of the Río Negro in northern Argentina, and in similar regions in Chile. Larger numbers of the geese graze on the Patagonian breeding grounds, where farmers accuse them of taking forage from sheep and contributing to the reduction of grass. Formerly, however, the geese grazed side by side with guanacos and the range did not deteriorate. It is not the geese but the overutilization of the range by the sheep that is causing the problem. When kept in balance, even the bleak, severe steppes of Patagonia demonstrate the productivity of which grasslands, worldwide, are capable.

Above, opposite. *The turkey vulture* (Cathartes aura) *is widespread in the Americas. It feeds on carrion, which it sights from high above. While searching for carcasses the vulture rides currents of hot air and circles repeatedly.*

Overleaf. *The guanaco* (Lama guanicoe) *is a member of the camel family. It is a herding animal, found both in mountains and on the pampas from Peru to the southern tip of South America.*

Picture Credits

Numbers correspond to page numbers.

Appendix

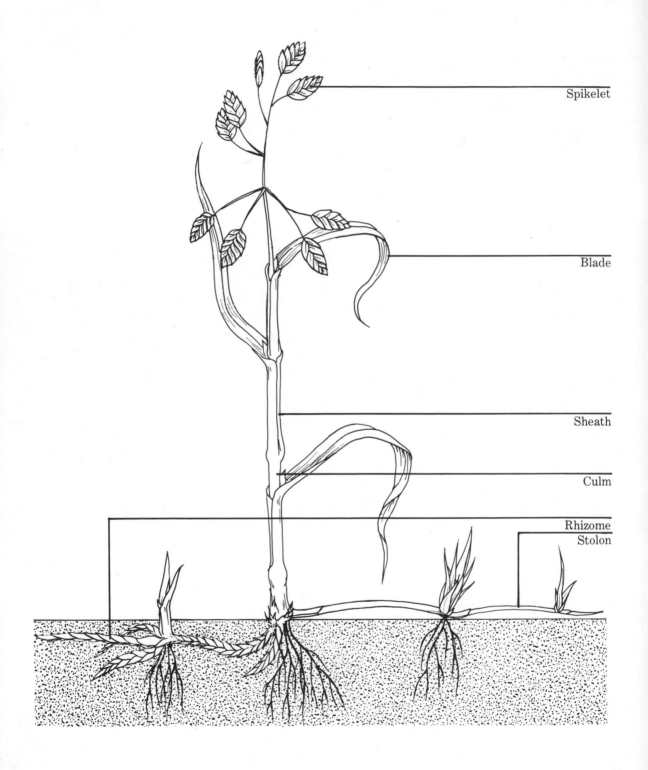

Spikelet

Blade

Sheath

Culm

Rhizome
Stolon

Members of the grass family (Gramineae) live from one to many years, but those that dominate grasslands are usually very long-lived. The erect stems, called culms, are usually prominently swollen at the region of the leaf attachment and are often hollow, except at the point of attachment. In addition, grasses may or may not produce horizontal stems, which are called rhizomes when they are below the ground surface and stolons when above. Grass leaves are alternate in their arrangement and often tend to line up approximately in two rows. Each leaf is clearly divided into a basal sheath, which tightly or loosely encloses a portion of the culm, and a spreading ribbon-like blade that may be flat, rolled, or folded. At the junction of the blade and sheath there is usually a small membrane or fringe of hairs called the ligule and sometimes also ear-like projections of the blade margins called auricles.

Grass flowers are arranged in very reduced spikes called spikelets, which are themselves borne in a variety of different kinds of clusters. Each spikelet bears one to many tiny flowers and a number of associated protective leaves or bracts. When spikelets bear more than one flower, the flowers are borne in two rows along a central axis called the rachilla. Each flower in a typical spikelet consists of a pistil with two feathery stigmas, which can be very effective at trapping wind-borne pollen, and three delicate stamens, whose anthers at maturity may dangle from the spikelet on thread-like filaments, shedding small clouds of pollen into the wind. The showy petals and protective sepals characteristic of insect-pollinated flowers are lacking in this family, but each little flower is normally protected by two special bracts, an outer one called the lemma and an inner one, the palea. For convenience the flower and its two associated bracts are collectively termed the floret. The floret or florets of a spikelet are usually also protected by two additional bracts called glumes. The florets of a spikelet may all contain both pistil and stamens or some or all of them may be unisexual or even sterile. The lemmas or the glumes or both may bear bristles, called awns, from their tips or their outer surfaces.

Flower

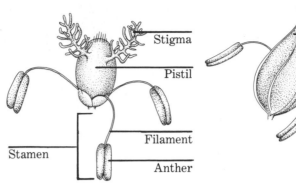

Stigma
Pistil
Stamen
Filament
Anther

Floret

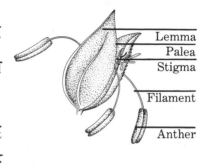

Lemma
Palea
Stigma
Filament
Anther

Membranous Ligule

Blade
Ligule
Auricles
Sheath

Fringed Ligule

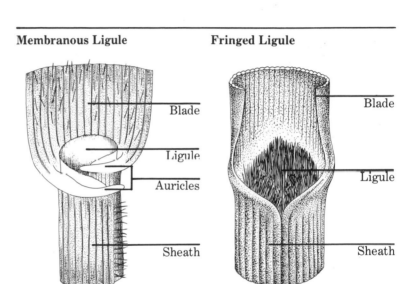

Blade
Ligule
Sheath

Spikelet with six florets

Awn
Rachilla
Lemma
First glume
Second glume

Spikelet with one floret

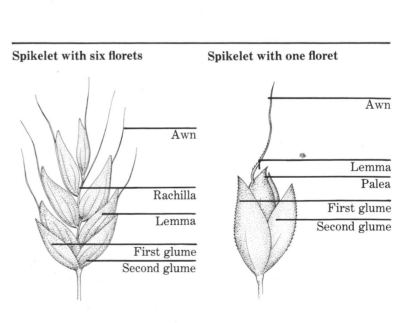

Awn
Lemma
Palea
First glume
Second glume

Avena fatua (60–80 cm)   **Calamagrostis canadensis** (60–120 cm)   **Deschampsia cespitosa** (20–120 cm)

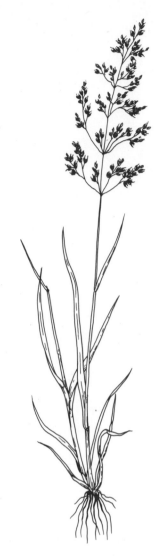

The grass family, because it is large and diverse, has traditionally been subdivided into smaller categories, called tribes, some of which are discussed and illustrated on the following pages. The tribe Aveneae, which is very large and diverse in temperate and cool regions, is defined principally by technical anatomical features, but it can often be recognized by its large glumes, which are usually longer than the florets, and by its much-branched spikelet clusters. The spikelets are rather variable, since they may contain from one to many florets and the lemmas of the florets may be awned or awnless.

Avena is a genus native to temperate Europe and Asia but widely cultivated and present elsewhere. It is easily recognizable because of its large spikelets and its lemmas, which often bear a prominent twisted and bent awn arising from the outer surface. Wild oats (Avena fatua) is closely related to the cultivated oats grown in temperate regions. Avena fatua is probably native to southern Europe, but it has become common elsewhere as a weed of cultivated and waste ground.

The genus Calamagrostis is distinctive because of the abundant long silky hairs which surround the base of the solitary floret. The lemma is usually awned, but the awn may be rather inconspicuous. Calamagrostis is found in both hemispheres, often in cool, moist places. Bluejoint (Calamagrostis canadensis) is widespread throughout northern North America in marshes, meadows, and open woods, and

Holcus lanatus (50–100 cm)   **Koeleria pyramidata** (20–60 cm)   **Phalaris arundinacea** (70–160 cm)

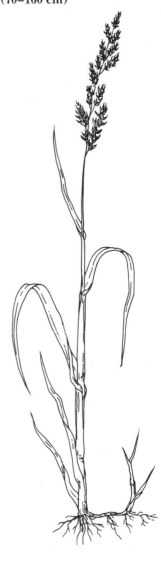

provides important forage for animals, both domestic and wild, in some regions.

Deschampsia is a genus of about 40 species of temperate, cool, and cold regions—there is even a species in Antarctica. Tufted hair grass (Deschampsia cespitosa) is found in cool environments throughout the world. It dominates extensive areas of montane grassland in some regions.

The genus Holcus comprises a small group of species native to Europe and Africa. Its spikelet cluster is characteristically rather condensed and its spikelets are two-flowered, with the upper floret relatively small and staminate or sterile. Velvet grass (Holcus lanatus) is native to Europe but has been widely introduced elsewhere as a meadow grass. It is suited to a wide range of

habitat from grassland to open woods and has become a weed in many localities.

Koeleria, a genus of perhaps 20 species in the temperate regions of both hemispheres, bears close similarities to the genus Poa of the tribe Festuceae, and so its placement in the Aveneae is uncertain, and there is considerable disagreement about the nomenclature of some of its species. June grass (Koeleria pyramidata) and its close relatives are important in grassland associations in Europe, Asia, Africa, and North America.

The genus Phalaris contains about 15 species in the temperate parts of Europe, Asia, Africa, and North and South America. It is sometimes placed in its own tribe rather than in the Aveneae because it has two tiny sterile

flowers below that remain attached to the solitary fertile one. Reed canary grass (Phalaris arundinacea) grows in moist places and in shallow water throughout most of the Northern Hemisphere. It may dominate extensive regions of wet ground and is often an important component of hay meadows.

197

Andropogon gerardii
(60–200 cm)

Andropogon scoparius
(40–100 cm)

Cymbopogon giganteus
(80–250 cm)

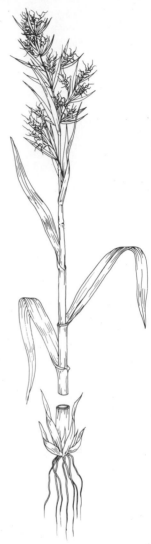

The tribe Andropogoneae is a large and important group that is most diverse in warm climates. It includes many of the dominant grasses of tropical and warm-temperate grasslands. The tribe is usually readily recognized because its spikelets are borne in pairs with one spikelet of each pair borne on a short stalk (or pedicel). The pediceled spikelet is usually somewhat smaller than the unstalked one and often staminate or sterile, while the other one is bisexual. Both spikelets have prominent glumes that are hard in texture and delicate, membranous lemmas and paleas. The best-developed spikelet usually has one sterile floret and one bisexual floret and the lemma of the fertile floret often possesses a prominent, twisted awn.

Andropogon *is an especially* important genus in the grasslands of North America, South America, and Africa. The name Andropogon, *derived from the Greek words for "man" and "beard," alludes to the usually bearded pedicels of the stalked spikelets. The two species illustrated here are both North American and both made up a significant part of the vegetation in the tallgrass and mixed prairies of the central part of the continent. Big bluestem* (Andropogon gerardii) *grows to about 2 meters in height and usually predominates in low, moist ground. Little bluestem* (Andropogon scoparius) *is much shorter and grows more abundantly on slopes and hilltops. Because its spikelet clusters are quite different from those of* Andropogon gerardii, Andropogon scoparius *is*

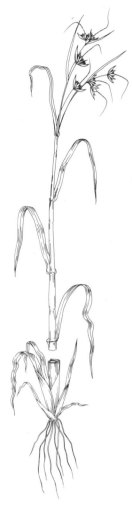

sometimes referred to a separate genus, Schizachyrium. Cymbopogon is a tropical and subtropical Old World genus, some of whose members are important in the African savannas. Various species are cultivated in warm climates for their useful aromatic oils and for their ornamental value. The species illustrated, giant oil grass (Cymbopogon giganteus) is a perennial up to 2.5 meters tall, found virtually throughout tropical Africa.

The genus Heteropogon is widespread but has relatively few species. Tanglehead (Heteropogon contortus) is found throughout the tropical and subtropical regions of the world, often in sandy grasslands. The awns of its spikelets are often twisted together into a pointed structure when young and may later become tangled into a knot-like mass. The florets, when they drop from the spikelets, are needle sharp on the base and may be injurious to grazing animals. Nevertheless, Heteropogon contortus is regarded in many regions as good forage when it is young.

Hyparrhenia is a genus native to the Old World tropics, but it has been widely introduced elsewhere. Hyparrhenia rufa grows throughout tropical Africa and is often a very important component of moist savannas. It is commonly planted as forage in the American tropics.

Themeda is also a significant genus in certain African grasslands, but kangaroo grass (Themeda australis) is native to Australia, where it is widespread, mostly in wooded habitats. It is especially distinctive when fully mature because it is tall and its fruiting parts have a conspicuous rusty-brown color.

199

Dichanthelium oligosanthes
(10–70 cm)

Echinochloa colonum
(10–70 cm)

Panicum virgatum (50–140 cm)

The Paniceae is a large tribe best represented in the warmer regions of the world. Its spikelets are two-flowered, each bearing one sterile or staminate floret and one bisexual floret. The glumes and the lemma of the lower floret are usually very similar to one another and rather soft in texture, while the lemma of the upper floret is firm or bony, with its margins inrolled over the palea.

Dichanthelium, often considered a subgenus of Panicum rather than a genus in its own right, is an American group of perennial grasses that undergo distinctive seasonal growth phases. Spring plants usually have a conspicuous terminal spikelet cluster and are unbranched. But later in the year the plants become highly branched and in summer and fall the spikelets are inconspicuous and borne among the branches. Scribner's dichanthelium (Dichanthelium oligosanthes var. scribnerianum) occurs throughout the United States in a large variety of habitats.

The genus Echinochloa is relatively small but very familiar, because some of its members are widespread as weeds. Most of its species are readily recognized because the leaf ligule, which is almost universally present in grasses, is absent. Jungle rice (Echinochloa colonum) is a weed of cultivated areas and damp ground throughout the tropics and subtropics.

Panicum is a very large and diverse genus of more than 500 species worldwide. Some of the species, for example Panicum maximum, are important forage

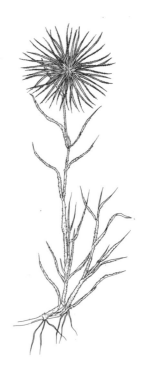

*grasses in the tropics. Switch
grass* (Panicum virgatum) *is
found throughout much of North
America and is often dominant in
wet prairies in the central United
States.*

The genus Paspalum *is made up
of about 400 species. Its spikelets
are distinctive because of their
dome shape and because they are
arranged in finger-like clusters
along flattened branches. Called
Dallis grass in the United States,*
Paspalum dilatatum *is a South
American species which has been
introduced throughout the tropics.
It prefers low, moist ground and
is considered a valuable forage
grass.*

Pennisetum *species are found in
the warm parts of both
hemispheres. They are easily
identified by the bristly
cylindrical spikelet clusters, with
each spikelet being attached to a*
*group of enclosing bristles when it
falls. Elephant grass* (Pennisetum
purpureum) *is found throughout
Africa along streams and in
moist, disturbed savanna or
forest. It is unusually robust,
attaining heights of 4 to 6 meters
when well grown. It has been
widely cultivated for forage and
building material.*

Hairy spinifex (Spinifex hirsutus)
*a sand-binding grass of temperate
coastal regions in Australia and
New Zealand, is interesting
because it forms plants of two
kinds—male and bisexual—and
because of the distinctive globular
spikelet cluster of the bisexual
plant. Spinifex is also the
common name of several prickly
grasses of other genera which
dominate the spinifex country of
central Australia.*

Astrebla pectinata (80–100 cm)   **Bouteloua curtipendula** (40–70 cm)   **Bouteloua gracilis** (10–50 cm)

In the tribe Chlorideae the spikelets are borne in one-sided spikes, the lemmas are three-nerved, and the ligule is usually a fringe of hairs. The tribe is confined mainly to warm regions, with a few important genera reaching farther north.

Astrebla *is a genus important in northern and eastern Australia in the regions known as Mitchell grass country.* Barley Mitchell grass (Astrebla pectinata) *together with* Astrebla squarrosa, Astrebla elymoides, *and species of* Aristida, Panicum, *and* Eragrostis, *dominates a tussocky grassland found on heavy clay soil.*

Bouteloua *is a diverse genus, most of whose members are in North America, but with a few representatives in Central and South America. Side oats grama* (Bouteloua curtipendula) *has* numerous short spikes, each of the spikes bearing relatively few spikelets and each falling as a unit from the plant at maturity. It is an important grass throughout the mixed and tallgrass prairie of central North America. Blue grama (Bouteloua gracilis) *falls into a different subgenus because it has a small number of long spikes, each of which bears numerous spikelets which break off individually above the glumes. It is important in both the mixed and shortgrass prairie and is often a dominant grass in the latter.*

The genus Buchloë *has only one species, buffalo grass* (Buchloë dactyloides) *This grass has separate staminate and pistillate plants; the staminate plants resemble a small species of* Bouteloua *but the pistillate plants have their spikelets aggregated*

Buchloë dactyloides (3–20 cm)   *Chloris gayana* (100–150 cm)   *Cynodon dactylon* (10–50 cm)

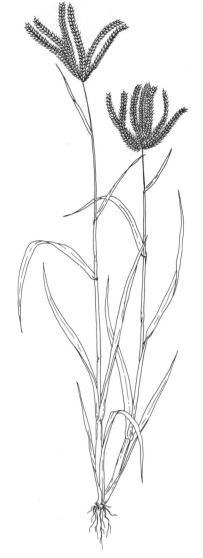
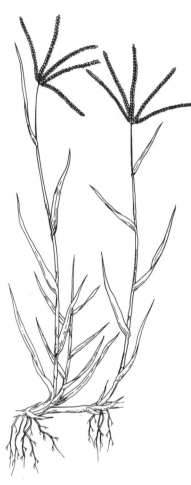

into small burr-like clusters.
Buchloë dactyloides *is short in*
stature, but it forms extensive
mats by virtue of its numerous
strong stolons. Like Bouteloua
gracilis, *it is important in the*
mixed and shortgrass prairie of
central North America and may
be dominant in the latter.
Buchloë, *because of its mat-*
forming ability and its low
moisture requirements, is gaining
favor as a lawn grass in arid
regions.
Chloris *is a relatively large genus*
found in warm climates. Its
spikelets have one to three
rudimentary or staminate florets
above a solitary perfect one.
*Rhodes grass (*Chloris gayana*) is*
cultivated as a forage grass in
warm regions.
The genus Cynodon *has a*
relatively small number of
species, but Bermuda grass

(Cynodon dactylon) *which may*
have originated in Africa, is
found around the world in
tropical and subtropical regions.
Because it forms dense mats,
even on poor soil, and can
withstand much mowing and
grazing, it is strongly favored as
a lawn and forage grass.

Bromus japonicus (20–60 cm) **Festuca ovina** (30–100 cm) **Poa pratensis** (10–100 cm)

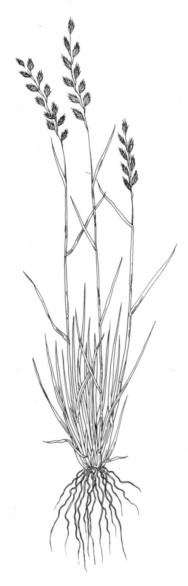

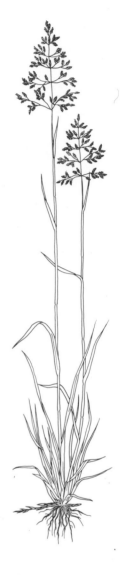

The Festuceae is a tribe of temperate and cool regions. Its spikelets have more than one floret, with the glumes unequal and usually shorter than the lowest lemma. The lemmas each have five or more nerves. Three of the largest genera—Bromus, Festuca, and Poa—are illustrated.

The genus Bromus is present in cool and temperate regions throughout the world. It can often be recognized by its large spikelets and by rather prominently veined lemmas that are usually somewhat divided at the tip and awned from just below the tip. Japanese brome (Bromus japonicus) is a common weed throughout much of the Northern Hemisphere.

Festuca is a fairly large genus found principally in cool and cold climates in both hemispheres.

Certain species are important components of the Eurasian steppes. The spikelets of Festuca are usually smaller than those of Bromus, and the lemmas are either awned or awnless and not as prominently veined. Sheep's fescue (Festuca ovina) is one of the most widespread species, being present in Asia, Europe, and North America. Several varieties of it are used as lawn grasses.

Many species have been described in the genus Poa, but many of these are difficult to distinguish, even for experts. The spikelets of Poa are smaller than those of Bromus, and although the lemmas are prominently veined, they are awnless. Characteristically, the leaf tip of Poa is shaped rather like the prow of a boat, a condition rarely found in other grass genera. Meadow bluegrass

Eragrostis cilianensis
(10–50 cm)

Muhlenbergia porteri
(30–100 cm)

Sporobolus pyramidatus
(10–60 cm)

(Poa pratensis) *is a common component of lawn mixtures sold in cool and temperate regions, and it is also popular as a pasture grass. Forms of it appear to be native to both the New World and the Old World.*
Members of the tribe Eragrosteae have one- to three-nerved lemmas and spikelets borne in branched clusters rather than in one-sided spikes; otherwise, the group is similar to the Chlorideae. Some authors prefer to unite the two tribes. Three genera of the Eragrosteae—Eragrostis, Muhlenbergia, *and* Sporobolus— *are illustrated.*
Eragrostis *is a very large genus of temperate and tropical regions. Roughly half of its species are weeds of disturbed ground, and some of these are very widespread. The spikelets of* Eragrostis *have three to many*

flowers and prominently three-nerved lemmas. The species illustrated, Eragrostis cilianensis, *is sometimes called stink grass because it has a distinctive, somewhat unpleasant odor. It is native to southern Europe but grows on waste ground in many parts of the world.*
The genus Muhlenbergia *is a relatively large genus, most of whose species are found in North and South America. Its florets are one-flowered with the lemmas awned or awnless and three-nerved. Bush muhly* (Muhlenbergia porteri) *is a distinctive species of dry regions in the southwestern United States and Mexico.*
Sporobolus *grows in temperate and tropical regions of both hemispheres. Its lemmas are awnless and one-nerved. Whorled dropseed* (Sporobolus

pyramidatus) *is found on sandy or saline soils in the southern United States and throughout tropical America.*

Agropyron smithii (50–90 cm)   *Elymus canadensis* (100–150 cm)   *Aristida adscensionis* (20–80 cm)

The tribe Hordeae is readily distinguished by the arrangement of the spikelets in two-sided spikes. Many of the genera in this tribe are somewhat controversial, being differently interpreted by different scholars. The genera Agropyron and Elymus are illustrated.

Agropyron is a genus of the cool and temperate regions of both hemispheres. Traditionally Agropyron is separated from Elymus because it has one spikelet at each node, while Elymus has two or three, but this distinction breaks down in some species, and some authors prefer to define the genera differently. Western wheatgrass (Agropyron smithii) is a rhizome-producing species found throughout much of the United States and Canada and is the dominant grass in certain cool prairies.

Elymus is a moderately large genus of the cool and temperate regions of the Northern Hemisphere. Canada wild rye (Elymus canadensis) is a variable and common species in much of the northern North America, occurring in a wide variety of habitats from open prairie to dense woodland.

The Aristideae is a small tribe of relatively few genera, readily distinguished by its solitary florets, each of which has a firm lemma with three awns or one three-branched awn at the tip. The genus Aristida contains about 200 species confined principally to the warmer parts of the world. Six-weeks three-awn (Aristida adscensionis) is one of the most widespread, being a common weed throughout the tropics and subtropics.

The tribe Oryzeae consists of a

number of genera adapted to moist habitats. The most obvious feature for its recognition is the absence of glumes (or the presence of only tiny, vestigial ones). The tribe is worldwide in its distribution, but relatively few species grow in temperate or cold regions. Oryza, Leersia, and Zizania are illustrated.

Oryza is a moderate–size genus of moist tropical habitats. Rice (Oryza sativa) is one of the world's most important cultivated crops. Occasionally it escapes and becomes weedy in suitable habitats.

Leersia is a small but widespread genus whose members grow in wet habitats in both temperate and tropical regions. Cutgrass (Leersia hexandra) is common near water in tropical and subtropical areas.

Zizania is a small genus of aquatic grasses with dramatic-looking spikelet clusters having staminate spikelets borne beneath pistillate ones. It grows only in temperate North America and eastern Asia. Wild rice (Zizania aquatica) produces grains that are highly prized as a gourmet food item. It is native to temperate North America but has been naturalized in the Soviet Union.

Oryzopsis hymenoides (30–80 cm)

Stipa capillata (20–70 cm)

Danthonia semiannularis (30–90 cm)

The Stipeae is a small but important tribe, distinguished by its one-flowered spikelets, by its rather bony, awned lemmas, and by a number of other anatomical features. The genera Oryzopsis and Stipa are illustrated. Oryzopsis is a relatively small genus with members in both hemispheres. It is closely related to Stipa, but the awn of Oryzopsis becomes detached from the mature lemma while that of Stipa remains attached. Indian rice grass (Oryzopsis hymenoides) is an important forage grass in dry regions of the western part of North America.

Stipa is a large and important genus almost worldwide in its distribution. Its twisted awn is usually very prominent, and its floret, when detached from the spikelet, is usually sharp-pointed at the base. Stipa capillata is one of the important species on the European steppes. Other species are important components of cool grasslands in North and South America.

The tribe Danthoneae is a relatively small group which is recognized, in part, by its two- to several-flowered spikelets, its two-pronged, awned lemmas, and its relatively long glumes. The genus Danthonia is a large one found everywhere in temperate regions but most diverse in the Southern Hemisphere. In Australia, a number of tussocky Danthonia species referred to as wallaby grass provide important forage, especially in southern regions. One such species is Danthonia semiannularis.

The Arundineae comprise a small number of sturdy genera with the spikelets arranged in large feathery clusters and bearing

silky hairs on or between the florets. The species illustrated, common reed (Phragmites australis) is virtually cosmopolitan. It grows around lakes, rivers, and streams and in marshes.

The tribe Aeluropodeae consists of a few genera which grow principally in alkaline soils. Most species produce stolons or rhizomes and have short, sharp-pointed leaves. In addition, there are several to many florets per spikelet, and the lemmas usually have seven or more nerves. In the genus Distichlis, the spikelets are unisexual, with the staminate and pistillate ones normally found on separate plants. Inland salt grass (Distichlis spicata var. stricta) is abundant on saline flats in the inland regions of North and South America. Although rather coarse and tough, it can provide important forage since it grows in regions where few other plants can.

The Unioleae is a small tribe whose members have large clusters of many-flowered spikelets with the uppermost and lowermost florets of each spikelet sterile. Sea oats (Uniola paniculata) is a striking coastal species of southern North America, the Bahamas, and the Caribbean islands.

Family Tree of the Artiodactyls

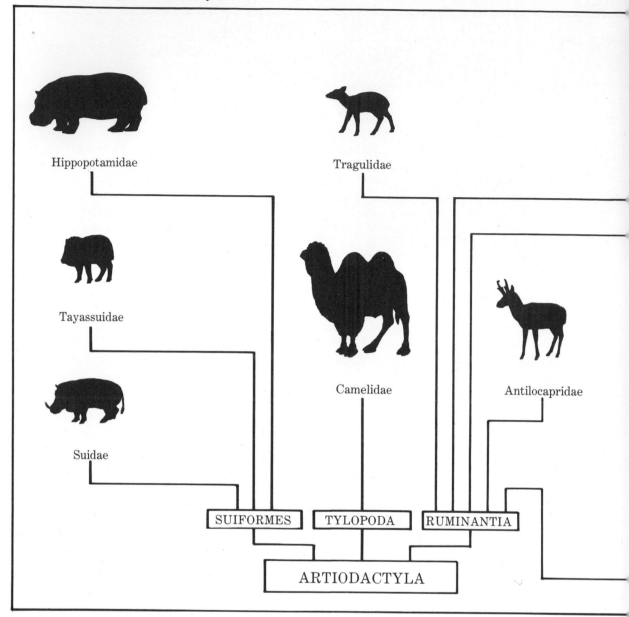

Hippopotamidae

Tragulidae

Tayassuidae

Camelidae

Antilocapridae

Suidae

SUIFORMES   TYLOPODA   RUMINANTIA

ARTIODACTYLA

Suidae: *Warthog*
Tayassuidae: *Collared peccary*
Hippopotamidae: *Hippopotamus*
Camelidae: *Bactrian camel*
Tragulidae: *Chevrotain*
Antilocapridae: *Pronghorn*
Cervidae, *left to right: Chinese
water deer, axis deer, mule deer*
Giraffidae: *Giraffe*
Bovidae, *left to right: top row
hartebeest, saiga, gerenuk, sable
antelope; bottom row gray duiker,
reedbuck, eland, wild yak*

*Artiodactyls are considered
among the most highly
evolved of mammals. The
order Artiodactyla is composed of
nine living families. Of these
families, the Suidae,
Tayassuidae, and
Hippopotamidae are closely
related and form a suborder of the
Artiodactyla known as the
Suiformes; these are the most
primitive and least specialized
members of the order. These
animals have simple 2- or 3-
chambered stomachs and are non-
ruminating.
The family Camelidae forms a
distinct suborder called
Tylopoda, all of whose members
have a 3-chambered, ruminating
stomach.
The Tragulidae, Cervidae,
Giraffidae, Antilocapridae, and
Bovidae are advanced
artiodactyls with complex, 4-*

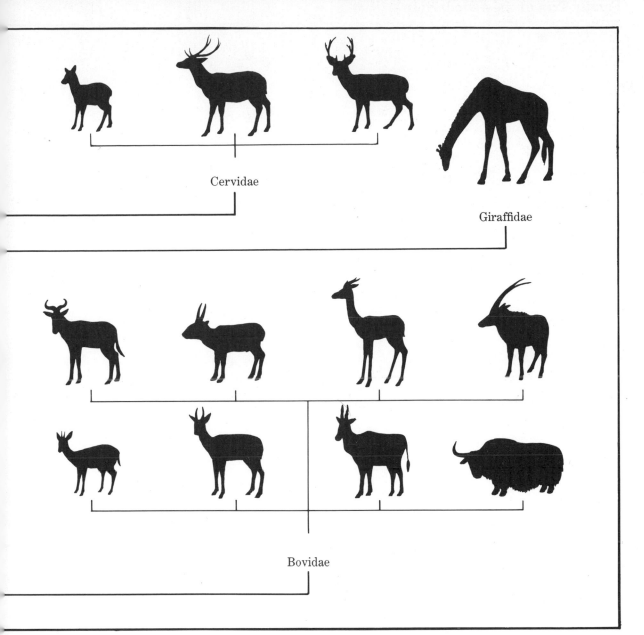

Cervidae

Giraffidae

Bovidae

chambered stomachs and true ruminating (cud-chewing) habits. They are classified in the suborder Ruminantia, and are not considered closely related to either the Suiformes or the Tylopoda. The family Bovidae is the dominant group of artiodactyls in the world in terms of number of species and total number of animals.

The families Cervidae and Bovidae differ from the other artiodactyls in that they are very large and contain species which differ widely from each other. They have, therefore, been subdivided by zoologists into subfamilies of more closely allied types. There are seven such subfamilies in the Cervidae, three of which are represented in the following text; a representative species of each of these three subfamilies is illustrated on the chart. Within the Bovidae, ten subfamilies are recognized, eight of which are represented in the text; a member species of each of these eight subfamilies is depicted in the chart above.

Artiodactyls of the Grasslands

*(Measurements, given in millimeters, correspond to the animals'
maximum shoulder height.)*

Phacochoerus aethiopicus
(850 mm)

Hylochoerus meinertzhageni
(1000 mm)

Camelus bactrianus (2100 mm)

Among the most conspicuous members of any grassland community are the even-toed ungulates or artiodactyls. Artiodactyls range from among the largest, most impressive of the world's mammals to tiny fleet-footed creatures that run at the least hint of danger. Scientists divide the artiodactyls into nine major groups, or families, most of which contain a few forms that are primarily adapted to grasslands. However, the true flowering of grassland artiodactyls has occurred in the major family Bovidae, and that flowering, as will be discussed later, is now most evident on the savannas of eastern and southern Africa.

The most primitive of the world's artiodactyls are generally considered to be the pigs (Suidae). Most artiodactyls have a "ruminating" stomach; the food is initially eaten rapidly with little chewing and then is regurgitated for more careful chewing and complete digestion at a later period. This ruminating habit of most artiodactyls makes them particularly suited to life in the grasslands, where the foods are low in nutrition and must be consumed in large quantities to provide adequate life support. In the pigs, however (and in the closely related peccaries), the stomach is 2-chambered, simple, and non-ruminating. Few species of pigs, and none of the peccaries, are, strictly speaking, grassland animals. Most pigs are omnivorous and consume many kinds of vegetable and animal matter. They live in a wide variety of habitats from the deep jungles and swamps of the tropics to the temperate forests of the north. Of the few forms that can be regarded as primarily grassland inhabitants, the warthog (*Phacochoerus aethiopicus*) is probably the best known. It is found all over subsaharan Africa outside of the forests, mountains, and deserts. To the human eye, the warthog is ugly in the extreme. Where it has any hair at all, it is thick and bristle-like. The head is very flattened and from its sides project the large warts that give the animal its name. These growths may serve to cushion blows from the tusks of rivals. The huge tusks are used to rake up the soil as the animal searches for the roots that form a major part of its diet. Other food items include grasses, berries, the bark of young trees, and occasionally carrion. This pig frequently seeks shelter on the savannas by backing into burrows dug by the aardvark (*Orycteropus afer*).

Another pig sometimes found in grasslands is the giant forest hog (*Hylochoerus meinertzhageni*). Although, as its name indicates, this animal occurs primarily in forests, it has been observed in the open grasslands of Albert National Park in Zaïre and is sometimes seen on the savannas of Kenya. The range of the species is central Africa, from Liberia in the west to Kenya in the east. It is a huge pig, with an exceptionally large, wide head. Oddly enough, despite its conspicuous size, the giant forest hog was not discovered until 1904. Even today, its distribution is not accurately known, probably because it inhabits only the wildest, most inaccessible regions. Usually this pig lives in family groups composed of a male, female, and 2 to 4 young. Family bonds are very strong. In contrast to the warthog, the giant forest hog is not a digger; roots and bulbs do not form a major part of its diet. Its food consists of grass, leaves, fruit, and other vegetation that it finds on the ground. The giant forest hog remains within a well-

Lama guanicoe (1300 mm)

Hydropotes inermis (550 mm)

Cervus porcinus (750 mm)

defined home range where it maintains numerous runways and bedding-down areas. Young are born at any time of the year, and are so vigorously defended by the parents that few fall to predators.

The camel family (Camelidae) is a very ancient one, and today has several grassland-adapted species. The family evolved 40 to 50 million years ago in North America and the fossil record shows that a vast range of camel-like creatures inhabited the continent until the Ice Age. About 2 million years ago, some of the camel-type animals migrated to Eurasia, where they evolved into the true camels that we know today.

Of the two Old-World species of camels surviving today, the one-humped or dromedary camel (*Camelus dromedarius*) is known only in its domesticated form. The two-humped or Bactrian camel (*Camelus bactrianus*) is still known from the wild, although its populations have been reduced to small remnants and its range is restricted to the Gobi Desert. Originally, the Bactrian camel inhabited the drier, grassy steppes of central Asia. In the 1850s, this species was reported to be so numerous that it was common to see dozens or even hundreds grazing together. After 1920, the Bactrian camel declined drastically because of persecution by humans for its meat and hides; it also was unable to compete with livestock for available food and water. This species is one of the largest artiodactyls, measuring almost 2 meters at the shoulder. Camels live in drier areas, both in lowlands and on high plateaus up to 2000 meters or more in altitude. In summer they move to the high altitudes, where they feed on grasses and scrub vegetation; in the winter they move back down to the lowland deserts, where they gather near oases. The Bactrian camel lives in herds of up to 20 or more females, led generally by a dominant male. It feeds on grasses, herbs, tree branches and leaves, and even on salty desert plants that other browsing animals completely reject; it is among the few animals that can drink brackish water, a valuable asset in the arid regions it inhabits.

The guanaco (*Lama guanicoe*) is also a member of the camel family and is found in the dry, open pampas in southern and western South America from sea level to altitudes of 4500 meters in the high mountains. It is the wild species that gave rise to both the domesticated alpaca and the llama, which have provided the Indians of South America with vital necessities such as meat, wool, and hides since earliest times. This animal lives in small herds of up to 20 females, kept together and guarded by a single male. The guanaco depends for safety on its sharp eyes, alertness, and great speed. It is a grazer, consuming almost exclusively the grasses that occur on the plains and mountain slopes where it lives. Loyalty is apparently well developed in this animal and it is reported that when the male leader of a herd is shot, the females often will not race away as might be expected, but rather will remain with him and attempt to nudge him to his feet. When fighting, males snap at each other's front legs in an effort to knock each other down, and cross necks, attempting to press one another to the ground. At such times they utter high-pitched screams changing to low growls.

Most members of the deer family (Cervidae) are woodland browsing animals. A few species, however, can be

Cervus axis (1000 mm)

Odocoileus hemionus (1050 mm)

Blastoceros bezoarticus
(750 mm)

described as adapted to grasslands, one among them being the Chinese water deer (*Hydropotes inermis*). This deer inhabits tall reeds, rushes, and grasses along rivers and on mountainsides in China and Korea. Unlike most deer, it has no antlers, males having long slender canines that extend well below the upper lip and which are as effective weapons of offense and defense as antlers would be. During the breeding season, fierce fights occur among males, who continually chase each other, uttering trilling and drumming sounds. When fighting for a female, these males stand head to head, each trying to put his head over the other's neck and slashing downward with his sharp canines. This neck fighting results in deep wounds and much loss of hair, but is seldom fatal. When pressed by predators, the water deer behaves much like a rabbit, remaining quiet and motionless in the grass, and running away only in the last second. It feeds on reeds, coarse grasses, and vegetables.

The axis deer (*Cervus axis*) and hog deer (*C. porcinus*) generally frequent open grasslands in India and Southeast Asia. The males of these beautiful deer possess large handsome antlers. They are brownish to bright rufous in coloration, and in the axis deer small white spots present a vivid contrast to the body coloration in summer pelage. The hog deer is often solitary, or at best congregates in groups of no more than two or three animals; the axis deer, on the other hand, is among the most gregarious of deer, often congregating in herds of as many as 100 or more animals composed of stags, does, and young of all ages. After the axis deer stag sheds his antlers in August, he retreats from the grassland into the jungle. There he grows a majestic new set of antlers, and when he rejoins the herd in the fall he is ready to do battle for a mate. During this period he may become especially dangerous, attacking not only other males but objects of all kinds. He dashes against trees and fences, plows his antlers into the ground, and threatens anyone and anything in the vicinity. These deer are grazers, feeding on grasses generally, but occasionally browsing among bushes and trees; they are also fond of fruit and flowers.

The mule deer (*Odocoileus hemionus*) is another of the few species of deer to be found in the grasslands. It generally avoids forests and woodlands and is usually found in open clearings with good grass cover. This animal is sometimes called the jumping deer because of its habit of jumping high off the ground and landing on all four feet. It is able to conceal itself very well in dense grass and brush, and often remains completely unnoticed by human observers close at hand. Social units usually consist only of a doe and her offspring of one or two years. Except during the fall mating season, males occur alone or in small groups of their own. During the winter, larger numbers of both sexes may congregate in favorable feeding areas. By the early twentieth century, the mule deer had almost been exterminated on the Great Plains of the United States, but careful regulation of hunting has since allowed it to become common again.

The pampas deer (*Blastoceros bezoarticus*) inhabits dry, open plains in Brazil, Paraguay, Uruguay, and northern Argentina. It is perhaps the most truly grassland species of deer, only occasionally being found in woodland. Originally the pampas deer used the tall pampas grass for

Giraffa camelopardalis
(3300 mm)

Antilocapra americana
(1100 mm)

Sylvicapra grimmia (670 mm)

cover, but with increasing settlement and cultivation, it has had to live more in the open and has become extremely wary. The pampas deer stag drops its antlers during the rut. The doe can have young at any time of the year. This species may be unique among deer in that the parents stay together after the young have been born. The dry open steppes which the pampas deer prefers are being turned more and more into grain fields, so that today this deer has been greatly reduced in numbers and has been eliminated except in the wilder and more desolate areas of its range.

The giraffe is a symbol of the African savanna. Although only two species of the family Giraffidae still exist, at one time the family was widespread over Europe and Asia and comprised numerous species, some with a bizarre appearance. The two living species, both African in distribution, are the okapi (*Okapia johnstoni*), a woodland inhabitant of the Ituri Forest, and the giraffe (*Giraffa camelopardalis*), which is spread all over tropical Africa in the drier savanna and bush; the giraffe strictly avoids heavy forest and jungle. The most obvious feature of the giraffe is its long neck; yet this animal has only seven neck vertebrae, like most other mammals. These vertebrae are, however, greatly elongated, and the long neck of the giraffe enables it to feed on the topmost branches of bushes and acacia trees that are normally out of the reach of other savanna animals. The giraffe is spotted brown on white in a complex pattern that camouflages it very well on the savanna. This animal often lives in loosely knit groups of about 2 to 10 animals, but herds of over 70 individuals have been observed. Most groups comprise one or more cows and their calves. Old bulls are often solitary but sometimes roam about with another bull to form a pair. The evenings and early mornings are spent searching for food, which consists almost entirely of leaves from trees and shrubs such as mimosa, acacia, and wild apricot. The giraffe is well adapted to the drier savannas in that it is able to go for many weeks at a time without water.

The pronghorn antelope (*Antilocapra americana*) is a typical inhabitant of the vast North American plains. It is the sole surviving representative of a family of hoofed animals (Antilocapridae) which dates back to the Middle Miocene in North America, and which at one time included a number of species with various types of branched horns and high-crowned molar teeth. Enormous numbers of pronghorns lived on the American prairies from the Mississippi River to the Rocky Mountains before the arrival of the pioneer settlers. They were almost as abundant as the bison (some estimates place their numbers at 40,000,000) and were slaughtered for food and "fun." Because of this intense persecution, the pronghorn was reduced by the beginning of the present century to 19,000 individuals and extinction of the species seemed imminent. Strict protection, however, has since been effective in halting the decline. The pronghorn has now recovered and is once again a prominent part of the western scene. During the spring and summer, individual male pronghorns establish territories within which they attempt to maintain groups of about 10 to 20 does. During the winter this social system breaks down, and both sexes gather in favorable areas in herds that may number 100 or

Gazella granti (890 mm)

Redunca redunca (950 mm)

Litocranius walleri (1050 mm)

more animals. The pronghorn is the fastest mammal on the American continent, being able to run at speeds in excess of 65 kilometers per hour. The species is unique among the world's horned animals; it annually sheds and renews the horn sheaths of its permanent horns. Both sexes have horns, and the period of shedding corresponds with the end of the social season.

The largest family of hoofed animals, and the one containing the greatest number of species adapted to life on the grasslands, is the Bovidae. Bovids differ from other hoofed animals in that they have horns throughout the year; the horns do not shed annually as in deer. The bovids include all the domesticated sheep and cattle as well as a host of wild species almost worldwide in distribution—the major regions of absence being South America and Australia—and varying in size from about 30 centimeters in height to over 2 meters.

The greatest concentration of bovids, both in number of species and individual animals, is found on the savannas of eastern and southern Africa. Of this vast assemblage of African bovids, one of the smallest is the gray duiker (*Sylvicapra grimmia*). This tiny animal is about 60 centimeters high at the shoulder and only a little over a meter in total length. It occurs in tropical southern Africa in areas with suitable grass cover, and occasionally at altitudes higher than those inhabited by any other antelope on the continent. It avoids dense forest but roams widely over the African bush steppe. It is predominantly nocturnal. The gray duiker travels singly or in pairs. It has great speed and stamina, usually being able to outdistance any dogs that may try to outrun it. In the daytime, it rests in scrub or grass and comes out to graze after sunset. Its diet is composed of almost any green plant that can be secured. The gray duiker is shy in the wild and has been noted in association with guinea fowl, which may act as sentinels for it. Most small and medium-sized predators feed on this duiker, including birds of prey and pythons; the duikers, however, are too small to be regularly pursued by the lion. In the African grasslands, the gray duiker occupies the niche of the small, fast, nocturnal creature and thus is able to actively compete with the host of large, diurnal hoofed animals that also find a home there.

The gazelles (*Gazella*) are among the most successful of the grassland and desert hoofed animals of northern Africa and Asia, numerous species and geographic races having evolved there over the ages. Today, about a dozen species are known to occur all across northern and eastern Africa, east to the plains of India and north into the Gobi Desert of Mongolia. These are medium-sized hoofed animals, measuring betweeen 65 and 95 centimeters in shoulder height. They frequent the plains and generally treeless areas from sea level to over 5200 meters in altitude. One of the better-known species is Grant's gazelle (*Gazella granti*), which lives in the open steppe and bush country of eastern Africa. During the dry season, these gazelles may gather in herds of 200 to 400 animals, whereas in the rainy season the huge herds break up into smaller ones. At this time, males become territorial and small groups of females stay with them for weeks or even months, roaming through the male's territory as "harem groups." Non-territorial males gather

Damaliscus dorcas (1100 mm)

Damaliscus lunatus (1300 mm)

Connochaetes gnou (1200 mm)

together in bachelor groups of their own. Migrating herds of Grant's gazelles move from higher to lower elevations or to new feeding grounds in the fall. At this time they move in a single file with the youngest and lowest-ranking animals walking ahead of the older males. Sometimes these migrating herds meet and the males from each group display intensely with each other. The displays are highly ceremonial and ritualized and seldom lead to serious injuries. Whether on the move or simply feeding in their vast numbers on the African savannas, members of the genus *Gazella* form a conspicuous part of the African grassland fauna and a major source of food for the large predators that share it with them.

The reedbucks (*Redunca*) comprise three species of medium-sized African bovids that live in rolling grassland, thin forest, and reed beds and along shores in subsaharan Africa. Only males have horns, which are distinctive: large at the base, prominently ringed, and curving gracefully backward and upward, with the tips pointing sharply forward. These bovids are not particularly gregarious. They usually live alone or in pairs or small family groups. They are early-morning and evening grazers, their diet consisting almost exclusively of the local grasses. They have been able to maintain their numbers fairly well, and none of the three species is regarded as endangered or threatened at the present time.

The gerenuk (*Litocranius walleri*) is a strange-looking hoofed animal of eastern Africa, where it lives in dry areas of thorn and shrub growth. The gerenuk is characterized by long slender legs, a long giraffe-like neck, and a very small wedge-shaped head. Males have horns; females do not. The species is a browser of vegetation of intermediate height, and it thus fills a niche somewhat between that of the high-browsing giraffe and the grazing animals which feed at ground level. The gerenuk lives alone or in small groups in which a single male may be closely guarded and protected by several females. The gerenuk is active throughout the day, feeding on leaves which it plucks with its long upper lip and tongue. To reach food it often stands upright with the forelimbs placed against the tree for support. The gerenuk is not a fast runner, preferring to seek protection by hiding behind bushes or trees and peeking around by means of its long neck.

The blesbok, topi, and bontebok (genus *Damaliscus*) are among the larger African artiodactyls, measuring over one meter in height at the shoulder. These animals inhabit grasslands and arid regions of subsaharan Africa; they avoid the deeply forested areas of central and western Africa. In the early days of the African explorers, thousands of these graceful antelopes were often seen grazing on the plains, but their numbers have now been greatly reduced through indiscriminate slaughter and extensive habitat disruption. The bontebok (*Damaliscus dorcas*) nearly became extinct and is listed by the United States government as endangered. The topi (*Damaliscus lunatus*) is regarded as among the fleetest of South African antelopes, but its usual gait is a lumbering canter. It sometimes lives in large herds comprising many females and one territorial bull. This large bull drives out the weaker bulls, which then form bands of their own.

Alcelaphus buselaphus
(1500 mm)

Hippotragus niger (1550 mm)

Hippotragus equinus (1600 mm)

Members of this genus are highly prized among hunters as trophies, and are much sought after as food. In South Africa, they have been semi-domesticated on ranches for hunting and food purposes for many years.

The black wildebeest (*Connochaetes gnou*) is widely distributed over the open grassy plains of South Africa. It is a large, heavily built animal with a long, flowing tail and a scraggly mane on the neck, shoulders, and throat. This animal was severely depleted by European settlers in South Africa who relentlessly shot it wherever it was found. Much of its habitat has been modified by livestock grazing and farming. It is now slowly recovering from near extinction and is found on many South African reserves and private farms where it is afforded protection. Socially, this wildebeest is divided into female herds of about 30 animals, small groups of bachelor males, and individual older males. The latter establish small territories which they vigorously defend against other males, and within which they attempt to control passing female herds. It has often been observed that wildebeest and other grassland animals in Africa not only are gregarious among themselves but associate with other species of animals as well. These associations are often beneficial, such as when a particularly nervous species, or individual, alerts the others to danger. For example, any animal which is in fast running flight automatically alerts others, which may then also take flight. By this means, all of the species in a grassland association may escape a dangerous predator.

The hartebeest (*Alcelaphus buselaphus*) at one time ranged over the entire African continent, from Egypt and North Africa to the Cape, and from Senegal in the west to Somalia in the east. Today it has been extirpated or is extremely rare in the northern and southern parts of this range, but is still widely distributed in Africa and often is the most common of the large antelopes in an area. It inhabits open plains or areas of scattered scrub, where it feeds primarily upon grasses. With its long, narrow head and sloping back, the hartebeest appears to be ungainly. But this impression disappears immediately when the animal flees across the plains with a springing, bouncing trot that can achieve great speed. As with the wildebeest, there are old territorial males, wandering groups of young males, and herds of females and calves.

The sable (*Hippotragus niger*) and roan (*H. equinus*) antelopes are large African bovids that are known for their magnificent curved horns. The sable antelope is somewhat smaller than the roan, and is more delicately built. It occurs in grassy and thinly forested savannas from Kenya to South Africa. The roan antelope is more widely distributed, occurring in savannas throughout subsaharan Africa. Both species are avidly sought as hunting trophies. The sable antelope usually associates in herds of 10 to 30 animals, but on occasion it is encountered in groups of up to 100 individuals. Generally these herds comprise females and young, with a single mature bull in attendance. Older bulls are usually solitary in nature. The roan antelope is found in smaller groups, usually consisting of 3 to 15 females and one adult male. In both species there also are groups of bachelor males which compete with one another and await the opportunity to take over a female herd. Roan and sable antelopes do not

Taurotragus oryx (1800 mm)

Syncerus caffer (1500 mm)

Bos mutus (2000 mm)

mingle with each other in areas where they both occur. Because of hunting pressure, both species have become wary of man. When closely pursued they are capable of speeds up to 55 kilometers per hour. The roan feeds exclusively on grasses and herbs that are on the ground and only rarely on the bushes and trees that are in the area. Both roan and sable antelopes can become savage and fierce when threatened, using their horns with amazing dexterity as weapons. When males fight during courtship, they have a ritualized behavior pattern: they fall onto their "knees" and threaten each other with their horns. They are among the few wild hoofed animals that, when pursued, will normally stand their ground and protect themselves with their horns.

The eland (*Taurotragus oryx*) is a massive ox-like animal characterized by heavy spiral horns which are present in both sexes. It occurs in grassy rolling country with brush and scattered trees in eastern and southern Africa. The eland is gregarious, being found on the plains in groups numbering from 5 to 70 animals; occasionally solitary bulls may be encountered. When alarmed the herd trots off with individuals usually in a single file, an old bull bringing up the rear. Its food consists of leaves, bushes, and succulent fruit which it breaks off with its long spiral horns. Males also use the horns to intimidate rivals during the mating season, and both sexes use them to drive away lions and cheetahs.

The African buffalo (*Syncerus caffer*) is one of the largest and most impressive of Africa's grassland animals. It is found everywhere south of the Sahara, usually near water and where there is sufficient cover. It is not only a creature of the grasslands; it also ranges widely into forested areas, even into the rain forest, and in the mountains to elevations of up to almost 3000 meters. The African buffalo is able to adjust to different environmental conditions as virtually no other African hoofed animal can. In the savannas of Africa, herds of females and young may number 50 to 2000 animals, but mature males temporarily form groups of 3 to 10. Generally speaking, the individual herds have no true leader, the role of leadership being assumed by any animal within the herd which is most familiar with the area through which the herd is passing, but there are separate hierarchies for males and females. The African buffalo herd is a true social unit and each individual finds within it the security and protection that is so necessary for its survival. The African buffalo is regarded as the most dangerous mammal in Africa, and probably has killed more big-game hunters than any other species on the continent. By nature, however, the buffalo is no more dangerous than any other wild animal, and human deaths have usually resulted from a lack of knowledge of the behavior of an injured buffalo rather than any innate viciousness of the animal.

Although the greatest number of species and individuals of the world's bovids are gathered on the African plains, as described above, a number of bovid species are characteristic of grasslands outside of Africa. Among the most prominent of these is the wild yak (*Bos mutus*), which is an inhabitant of the montane grasslands of the Tibetan plateau. This huge animal may stand as high as 2 meters at the shoulders and weigh well over 450 kilograms. It prefers high elevations, up to 6000 meters in

Bubalus arnee (1800 mm)

Bison bison (2000 mm)

Antilope cervicapra (800 mm)

altitude, in the wildest and most desolate surroundings. The horns are large and black and curve upward and forward in the males. Long, shaggy hairs hang down all over the body to form a fringe around the shoulders and sides. Most of the year, cows and calves associate in large herds, while bulls gather in small groups of two or three animals. The yak, for all its size and weight, is a surefooted and sturdy climber. In Tibet, it has been domesticated for centuries, providing a good source of milk and meat; it also is used there as a beast of burden. Unfortunately, wild populations are now considered endangered because of excessive hunting.

The Asiatic water buffalo (*Bubalus arnee*) is found as a domesticated animal throughout southern Asia, from Egypt to the Philippines. In the wild, it is found in parts of India, Nepal, Sri Lanka, Indochina, and (through introduction) northern Australia in dense grass and reed growth in moist areas. This is another huge ox-like animal, weighing well over 650 kilograms and possessing the largest horns of any bovid, sometimes measuring nearly 1.5 meters in spread across the outer edges. This species generally is associated with large rivers and their tributaries in the riverain grass jungles and marshes, but has been widely eliminated through human settlement and the clearing and cultivation of land. It is also extensively hunted for meat, hides, and horns. As with the African buffalo, there are large herds of females and calves, sometimes including several hundred animals, and smaller separate groups of males. During the wet season the males join the female herds and mating occurs. A dominant female seems to lead each group, even when males are present. Water buffaloes and Indian rhinoceroses often graze adjacent to each other in complete toleration. If a rhino comes too close to a buffalo, the buffalo withdraws quietly and slowly and without any sign of excitement. By contrast, however, elephants seem to avoid water buffaloes wherever the two occur in the same vicinity.

The American bison (*Bison bison*) is another animal, like the pronghorn, that was a symbol of the American Great Plains before the coming of the settlers. At that time, the number of bison occurring on these grasslands was staggering. In 1871, competent witnesses reported seeing an enormous gathering of bison on the Arkansas River that must have numbered more than 4,000,000 animals. These animals formed a herd that was 80 kilometers deep and 40 kilometers wide, and this was only one of numerous herds in existence at that time. It is estimated that more than 50,000,000 bison once roamed the North American prairie, but by 1889 there were only 541 left. They had been shot and otherwise persecuted to the point of extinction, and only the timely intervention of some dedicated conservationists brought a halt to the slaughter and caused measures to be instituted which protected the pitiful remnants. As a result of these efforts, the bison is today well protected in a number of national parks and private preserves in North America.

The blackbuck (*Antilope cervicapra*) is found in the grasslands of India. It lives in open plains throughout the subcontinent and avoids hilly and forested areas. This animal is of special interest for two reasons. The horns, which are found in the bucks only, are extremely long (up

Procapra gutturosa (750 mm)

Procapra picticaudata (620 mm)

Saiga tatarica (800 mm)

to almost a meter in length), round in section, and twisted spirally up to five turns. These horns are impressive and unique weapons for a medium-sized bovid. Secondly, the blackbuck is one of the few hoofed animals in which males and females differ completely in coloration. The buck is a rich dark brown on the back and sides whereas the doe is a yellowish fawn; both sexes are whitish underneath and have a white ring encircling the eye. This bovid lived in small bands of from 15 to 50 animals, including several mature males which competed for control of the females, but in the present time herds are much smaller. Bucks which have not succeeded in gathering a herd of females live in groups by themselves. The shortgrasses typical of the plains of India are its chief food.

On the grassy plains of Mongolia, Tibet, China, and Siberia are found two species of bovids known as the Mongolian (*Procapra gutturosa*) and Tibetan (*P. picticaudata*) gazelles. The Tibetan gazelle ranges in the mountain meadows up to altitudes of 5500 meters and more. Only the males in these species have horns, which have a pronounced backward curvature, reminiscent of the horns of some breeds of domestic goats. The sexes of the Mongolian gazelle live in separate herds except during the spring mating season when they migrate to better pastures. At this time, very large herds of 6000 to 8000 individuals may be encountered. On reaching the summer pastures, the sexes separate and the young are born; the sexes remain apart until the rutting season begins in the fall. The Tibetan gazelle travels singly or in pairs and scattered groups. Both species are extremely wary and swift-running, but are often pursued by hunters for their meat and hides.

One of the most typical of the grassland animals of the world is the saiga (*Saiga tatarica*) of Russia; it is also one of the most bizarre in appearance. The remarkable feature of the animal is the inflated and trunk-like nose with downward-pointing nostrils. Such a huge proboscis is unknown among other bovids and it may be an adaptation for warming and moistening the cold, clear air of the treeless steppes on which the saiga lives. In the fall the saigas gather in large herds to migrate southward to warmer grassy areas. In the spring the herds split into small mating groups of from 2 to 6 animals, and later in the summer they reassemble into large herds. The saiga is an extremely fast runner, its speed having been clocked in excess of 65 kilometers per hour. Food for this animal is almost exclusively the grasses of the steppes, which also provide sufficient water so that the species can subsist for long periods of time without drinking. During the Ice Age the saiga roamed the steppes of Europe and Asia from England, through Germany and Russia, to as far as Siberia and even Alaska. In recent times the species was found from Poland to the Caucasus and the Caspian Sea. But through ruthless hunting to obtain their horns (they were highly prized by the Chinese as an aphrodisiac), the saigas were practically wiped out; by 1920 only a few thousand were left. Subsequently, strict control of hunting allowed the herds to again increase in numbers, and today over 2 million saigas roam the steppes. The remarkable recovery of this species gives cause for hope that artiodactyls will continue to flourish on the grasslands of the world for many years to come.

Glossary

Agamid. A member of the Agamidae, a lizard family of suborder Sauria, mostly found in tropical regions of the Old World and Australia and which includes the thorny devil (*Moloch horridus*) and the agamas (*Agama*).

Antelope. A common name which covers many grazing or browsing mammals of the family Bovidae. Most antelopes are slender animals found on African grasslands. The pronghorn of western North America is also called an antelope, although it is only distantly related to the antelopes of the Old World.

Arboreal. Pertaining to the tree habitat; living in trees.

Bovid. A member of the Bovidae, a family of hoofed ruminant mammals of the order Artiodactyla, including goats, cattle, sheep, African and Asian antelopes, the American pronghorn, and bison. Domestication of bovids is thought to have begun in Asia approximately 8000 years ago.

Browser. An animal that feeds on leaves and young shoots of trees and shrubs. See Grazer.

Caatingas. A South American term for thorn forest; a region of dry, warm climate dominated by a dense growth of small, thorny deciduous trees.

Camouflage. Pattern, shape, and color that renders an organism less conspicuous to a predator or to prey.

Campo. (from Spanish) In South America, a relatively level plain with scattered trees.

Campo cerrado. (from Spanish) A rolling semiarid grassland of northeastern South America, typically with poor soils and only occasional trees.

Canid. A member of the Canidae, a family of mammals of the order Carnivora, including dogs, wolves, foxes, and jackals. Canids are characterized in part by non-retractable claws and by teeth adapted for shearing.

Carnivore. 1. Any flesh-eating animal. 2. A member of the order Carnivora, a large group of mammals which includes bears, cats, dogs, hyenas, raccoons, skunks, and mongooses. Some authors also include seals and walruses in this order.

Carrion. Dead, often decomposing, animal flesh.

Climax community. The final, self-perpetuating stage of succession attained by a plant community under the particular environmental conditions present at a particular place and time. The stages of development leading up to the climax community are called successional or seral stages.

Covey. A small flock of quail or similar birds.

Crepuscular. Of or like twilight; active at twilight.

Deciduous forest. A forest composed mostly of broad-leaved flowering trees that shed all their leaves at a particular season. In a temperate deciduous forest, this occurs during the winter; in a tropical deciduous forest, during the dry season.

Deer. Even-toed hoofed mammals of the family Cervidae in the order Artiodactyla. Most cervids possess antlers. The Cervidae include elk, moose, and caribou.

Desert. A dry region with sparse plant cover. Often the rainfall is less than 10 cm. per year.

Diurnal. Daily; active during the daytime.

Dry savanna. A savanna transitional to desert or semi-desert. Characteristically, the vegetation is a mixture of thorny trees or shrubs and both tall and short grasses. See Savanna.

Edentate. A member of the order Edentata, a group of mammals that includes sloths, armadillos, and anteaters. Although "edentate" means "without teeth," some species do have cheek teeth (molars). Incisors and canine teeth are absent in all members. Most edentates feed upon soft-bodied insects, but the sloths are herbivorous.

Equine. Horselike.

Glade. A small open space in a forest.

Grain. The fruit of the grass family, consisting of a single seed enclosed by and adhering to the persistent ovary wall.

Grassy savanna. A savanna in which trees are few and widely spaced. See Savanna.

Grassy steppe. A central steppe region of Eurasia, a region bordered by wooded steppe on the north and by drier steppe (transitional to desert) on the south. See Steppe.

224

Grazer. An animal which feeds upon leaves and shoots of herbaceous vegetation, especially grasses. See Browser.

Gular sac. In certain birds, a pouch in the throat region that may be inflated with air or used as a food receptacle.

Herbivore. An animal that subsists principally on plant food.

Hibernation. 1. A state of reduced metabolic activity and lowered body temperature which occurs in some mammals as an adaptation to cold. 2. Winter dormancy in vertebrate animals.

High plains. See Shortgrass prairie.

Humidity. The amount of water vapor in the air.

Lateritic soil. A soil type rich in iron oxide, formed mainly in tropical regions from many kinds of rock that weather in strongly oxidizing and leaching conditions. Typically, it is soft, clay-like, and porous, but becomes very hard when exposed.

Llanos. (from Spanish) A grassland region of northern South America, occupying parts of Venezuela and Colombia, with trees along the watercourses and scattered xerophytic trees in the higher ground.

Mahout. (from Hindi) One who drives or trains elephants.

Maidan. (from Persian) A grassy, open area near a town. A glade.

Mallee scrub. Scrub vegetation of southern

Australia in which most conspicuous plants are shrubs of the genus *Eucalyptus.*

Marsupial. A member of the order Marsupialia, the pouched mammals, including the opossums, kangaroos, koalas, and wombats. Most modern marsupials are found in Australia, with some representatives in the Americas. The only marsupial in North America is the opossum.

Merychippus. An extinct genus of small horses whose fossils are found in middle and upper Miocene deposits. In some types, three toes remained large, but other types had the lateral toes much reduced.

Midgrass prairie. A prairie region occupied by a mixture of grasses of short and intermediate height, seldom more than 1 meter tall. The major type of prairie found in the Great Plains region of North America, occupying the space between the shortgrass prairie and the tallgrass prairie.

Miocene epoch. A division of geologic time which began about 26 thousand years ago. It follows the Oligocene epoch and precedes the Pliocene epoch.

Miombo. Local word for woodland in Tanzania.

Mitchell grass. A common name for several species of the grass genus *Astrebla,* an important component of eastern and northern Australian grasslands.

Monitor. A lizard of the family Varanidae. Most monitors live in the Old World tropics and subtropics. Several species attain great size and length.

Monsoon forest. Open woodlands that form in warm regions with prolonged dry periods followed by heavy rainfall. Also called tropical deciduous forest because the trees usually come into leaf only during the wet season.

Monte. (from Spanish) A semiarid region of Argentina in which the vegetation is dominated by woody, xerophytic shrubs.

Mulga scrub. Scrub vegetation of Australia in which the most conspicuous woody plant is the mulga (*Acacia aneura*).

Nocturnal. Of the night; active at night.

Pampas. (from Quechua Indian) A plain extending from central Argentina to the Andean foothills bounded by Patagonia on the south and the Gran Chaco on the north.

Pantanal. The flood plain along the east bank of the upper Paraguay River in southwest Brazil.

Pelage. The furry coat of a mammal.

Plains. Open areas of flat topography, often covered with relatively short grasses.

Pluvials. Long periods of heavy precipitation in some areas of the subtropics, corresponding to periods of glacial advance in the temperate zones.

Population. Any group of organisms, usually of a single species.

Prairie. Common name for open grassland, especially that of central North America.

Predator. An animal that kills and feeds upon other animals.

Pride. A group, especially of lions.

Puszta. (from Hungarian) A common name for the steppe of central Europe.

Rain forest. Common term for wet forest, especially for tropical forest dominated by broad-leaved evergreen trees, but also including wet temperate coniferous forest.

Raptor. A bird of prey, such as an eagle, hawk, falcon, and osprey, or owl.

Rhizome. An underground stem found in some perennial plants. It produces both shoots and roots and serves to spread the plant vegetatively.

Rodent. A member of the large order Rodentia, which includes the gnawing mammals such as rats, mice, prairie dogs, voles, porcupines, squirrels, beavers, and agoutis. All rodents have self-sharpening, ever-growing incisor teeth.

Ruminant. A member of the suborder Ruminantia in the order Artiodactyla, a group of mammals in which food is swallowed, passed into a storage stomach (rumen), returned to the mouth for further chewing, and then sent through the rest of the digestive tract. The group includes cattle, sheep, goats, deer, camels, giraffes, and antelopes.

Sagebrush. A North American common name for

several shrubby, aromatic, silvery-leaved species of the genus *Artemisia*.

Savanna. 1. Any tropical or subtropical grassland which has scattered trees or shrubs. 2. Any grassland with scattered woody vegetation. 3. Any African grassland.

Scavenger. An animal that subsists mainly on carrion or dung.

Scrub. A term often applied to a type of vegetation dominated by low, often thick-leaved, shrubby plants.

Semi-desert. A region transitional between grassland and desert.

Shortgrass prairie. Prairie dominated by grasses less than 20 centimeters tall; usually applied to the North American high plains region, which is dominated by members of the genera *Buchloë* and *Bouteloua* and is located along the east flank of the Rocky Mountains.

Specialized. Having specific adaptations to a particular environment or way of life.

Species. A population of one kind of organism whose members are at least potentially able to interbreed with each other but that are reproductively isolated from other populations.

Spinifex grasslands. Dry grasslands of east-central Australia that are dominated by a number of species of tough, prickly grasses, especially of the genus *Triodia*.

Steppe. Dry grassland dominated by grasses of the

genera *Stipa* and *Festuca*. The principal regions of steppe are in central Eurasia.

Stolon. A horizontal stem above or resting on the surface of the ground. Like the rhizome, it serves to spread the plant.

Succulent. A plant with thick, fleshy leaves or stems containing abundant water-storage tissue. Cacti and stonecrops are examples.

Symbiosis. A term describing a relationship between two species, commonly applied to a relationship of mutual benefit, but also used in a much broader sense to encompass all types of positive and negative associations.

Tallgrass prairie. Prairie dominated by grass species more than 1 meter tall, usually referring to the easternmost North American prairie, whose lowland regions were dominated by big bluestem (*Andropogon gerardii*). Also called True prairie.

Termitary. A termite nest.

Territory. The part of an animal's home range that is defended for purposes such as nesting, mating, roosting, or feeding.

Tiller. In the grass family, a ground-level lateral shoot similar to a stolon or rhizome, but short and nearly erect.

True prairie. See Tallgrass prairie.

Ungulate. A commonly used word for a hoofed mammal, including all members of the orders Perissodactyla and Artiodactyla. The term has no taxonomic status.

Veldt. A common term for open country in southern Africa, often dominated by open grassland or savanna.

Wallaby grass. A common name for a number of clump-forming species of the genus *Danthonia* which are important Australian grasses, especially in the south.

Wooded savanna. A savanna in which trees are abundant; a region transitional to a forest.

Wooded steppe. The northernmost steppe region of Eurasia; a region transitional between open steppe and forest.

Index

Page numbers in bold face type indicate illustrations